A Note From Rick Renner

I0165282

I am on a personal quest to see a "revival of the Bible" so people can establish their lives on a firm foundation that will stand strong and endure the test when the end-time storm winds begin to intensify.

In order to experience a revival of the Bible in your personal life, it is important to take time each day to read, receive, and apply its truths to your life. James tells us that if we will continue in the perfect law of liberty — refusing to be forgetful hearers but determined to be doers — we will be blessed in our ways. As you watch or listen to the programs in this series and work through this corresponding study guide, I trust that you will search the Scriptures and allow the Holy Spirit to help you hear something new from God's Word that applies specifically to your life. I encourage you to be a doer of the Word that He reveals to you. Whatever the cost, I assure you — it will be worth it.

> Thy words were found, and I did eat them;
> and thy word was unto me the joy and rejoicing of mine heart:
> for I am called by thy name, O Lord God of hosts.
> — Jeremiah 15:16

Your brother and friend in Jesus Christ,

Rick Renner

Unless otherwise indicated, all scripture quotations are taken from the *King James Version* of the Bible.

Scripture quotations marked (*AMPC*) are taken from the *Amplified® Bible*. Copyright © 1954, 1958, 1962, 1964, 1965, 1987 by The Lockman Foundation. Used by permission. **www.Lockman.org**.

Scripture quotations marked (*NIV*) are taken from *Holy Bible, New International Version®, NIV®* Copyright ©1973, 1978, 1984, 2011 by Biblica, Inc.® Used by permission. All rights reserved worldwide.

Scripture quotations marked (*TLB*) are taken from *The Living Bible* copyright © 1971. Used by permission of Tyndale House Publishers, Inc., Carol Stream, Illinois 60188. All rights reserved.

Symbols of the Holy Spirit

Copyright © 2020 by Rick Renner
8316 E. 73rd St.
Tulsa, Oklahoma 74133

Published by Rick Renner Ministries
www.renner.org

ISBN 13: 978-1-68031-748-0

eBook ISBN 13: 978-1-68031-749-7

All rights reserved. No portion of this book may be reproduced or transmitted in any form or by any means — electronic, mechanical, photocopy, recording, scanning, or other — except for brief quotations in critical reviews or articles, without the prior written permission of the Publisher.

How To Use This Study Guide

This ten-lesson study guide corresponds to *"Symbols of the Holy Spirit" With Rick Renner* (Renner TV). Each lesson in this study guide covers a topic that is addressed during the program series, with questions and references supplied to draw you deeper into your own private study of the Scriptures on this subject.

To derive the most benefit from this study guide, consider the following:

First, watch or listen to the program prior to working through the corresponding lesson in this guide. (Programs can also be viewed at **renner.org** by clicking on the Media/Archives links.)

Second, take the time to look up the scriptures included in each lesson. Prayerfully consider their application to your own life.

Third, use a journal or notebook to make note of your answers to each lesson's Study Questions and Practical Application challenges.

Fourth, invest specific time in prayer and in the Word of God to consult with the Holy Spirit. Write down the scriptures or insights He reveals to you.

Finally, take action! Whatever the Lord tells you to do according to His Word, do it.

For added insights on this subject, it is recommended that you obtain Rick Renner's books *Why We Need the Gifts of the Holy Spirit* and *The Holy Spirit and You: Working Together as Heaven's "Dynamic Duo."* You may also select from Rick's other available resources by placing your order at **renner.org** or by calling 1-800-742-5593.

TOPIC

The Holy Spirit in Action

SCRIPTURES

1. **Genesis 1:1,2** — In the beginning God created the heaven and the earth. And the earth was without form, and void; and darkness was upon the face of the deep. And the Spirit of God moved upon the face of the waters.

2. **Luke 1:34,35** — …How shall this be, seeing I know not a man? And the angel answered and said unto her, The Holy Ghost shall come upon thee, and the power of the Highest shall overshadow thee: therefore also that holy thing which shall be born of thee shall be called the Son of God.

3. **Matthew 3:16** — And Jesus, when he was baptized, went up straightway out of the water: and, lo, the heavens were opened unto him, and he saw the Spirit of God descending like a dove, and lighting upon him.

4. **John 3:34 (*TLB*)** — …For God's Spirit is upon him without measure or limit.

5. **Acts 1:8** — But ye shall receive power, after that the Holy Ghost is come upon you: and ye shall be witnesses unto me both in Jerusalem, and in all Judaea, and in Samaria, and unto the uttermost part of the earth.

6. **Acts 2:4** — And they were all filled with the Holy Ghost, and began to speak with other tongues, as the Spirit gave them utterance.

7. **Acts 4:31** — And when they had prayed, the place was shaken where they were assembled together; and they were all filled with the Holy Ghost, and they spake the word of God with boldness.

8. **Acts 5:14-16** — And believers were the more added to the Lord, multitudes both of men and women. Insomuch that they brought forth the sick into the streets, and laid them on beds and couches, that at the least the shadow of Peter passing by might overshadow some of them. There came also a multitude out of the cities round about

unto Jerusalem, bringing sick folks, and them which were vexed with unclean spirits: and they were healed every one.

9. **Acts 6:8** — And Stephen, full of faith and power, did great wonders and miracles among the people.

10. **Acts 8:5-8** — Then Philip went down to the city of Samaria, and preached Christ unto them. And the people with one accord gave heed unto those things which Philip spake, hearing and seeing the miracles which he did. For unclean spirits, crying with loud voice, came out of many that were possessed with them: and many taken with palsies, and that were lame, were healed. And there was great joy in that city.

11. **Acts 10:44,45** — While Peter yet spake these words [the Gospel], the Holy Ghost fell on all them which heard the word. And they of the circumcision which believed were astonished, as many as came with Peter, because that on the Gentiles also was poured out the gift of the Holy Ghost.

12. **John 16:13** — Howbeit when he, the Spirit of truth, is come, he will guide you into all truth: for he shall not speak of himself; but whatsoever he shall hear, that shall he speak: and he will shew you things to come.

13. **Acts 11:28-30** — And there stood up one of them named Agabus, and signified by the Spirit that there should be great dearth throughout all the world: which came to pass in the days of Claudius Caesar. Then the disciples, every man according to his ability, determined to send relief unto the brethren which dwelt in Judaea: which also they did, and sent it to the elders by the hands of Barnabas and Saul.

14. **Acts 13:2** — As they ministered to the Lord, and fasted, the Holy Ghost said, Separate me Barnabas and Saul for the work whereunto I have called them.

15. **Acts 14:10** — Said with a loud voice, stand upright on thy feet. And he leaped and walked.

16. **Acts 19:6 (*NIV*)** — ...The Holy Spirit came on them, and they spoke in tongues and prophesied.

17. **Acts 19:11-12** — And God wrought special miracles by the hands of Paul: so that from his body were brought unto the sick handkerchiefs or aprons, and the diseases departed from them, and the evil spirits went out of them.

GREEK WORDS

1. "power" — δύναμις (*dunamis*): the New Testament word for explosive power; used to describe the full might of an advancing army

SYNOPSIS

The ten lessons in this study on *Symbols of the Holy Spirit* will focus on the following topics:

- The Holy Spirit in Action
- The Holy Spirit — Oil and Dew
- The Holy Spirit — Rain, River, Water
- The Holy Spirit — Fire, Dove, Clothing
- The Holy Spirit — Wind
- The Holy Spirit — Gift
- The Holy Spirit — Seal and Earnest
- The Holy Spirit — Glory and Light
- The Holy Spirit — Wine
- 15 Symbols of the Holy Spirit

The emphasis of this lesson:

When the restrictions are lifted and the Holy Spirit is allowed to move, He produces mighty, supernatural acts in our lives, our churches, and our communities.

If there is one word that really helps communicate who the Holy Spirit is, it is the word "action." All throughout Scripture — from Genesis to Revelation — we see that when the Spirit of God is given freedom to move and do what He wants to do, supernatural things take place.

Andrew Murray — a nineteenth century pastor, teacher, and prolific author from South Africa — said, "Men ought to seek with their whole hearts to be filled with the Spirit of God. Without being filled with the Spirit, it is utterly impossible that an individual Christian or a church can ever live or work as God desires."

One reason we don't see more supernatural activity in the Church today is because we have restricted the movement of the Holy Spirit. In order to see and experience the power of God in operation, including the manifestation of the gifts of the Spirit, we have to allow the Holy Spirit to freely move in our lives.

The Holy Spirit Moved in Old Testament Times

From the very beginning of Scripture, the Holy Spirit is present and actively involved in the world. In fact, He is first mentioned in Genesis 1:1 and 2. The Bible says, "In the beginning God created the heaven and the earth. And the earth was without form, and void; and darkness was upon the face of the deep. And the Spirit of God moved upon the face of the waters."

It is important to note that the first mention of any recurring theme, principle, or person in Scripture is significant because it establishes a precedent. In this case, we see that the very first time the Holy Spirit is mentioned, He is not silent nor is He stationary. He is *moving*. And whenever the Holy Spirit is allowed to move, He does miraculous and amazing things. In verse 2, we see that the earth was without form and void, and darkness was upon the face of the deep. But when the Holy Spirit moved, creative power was released, and suddenly order was brought to chaos.

The truth is, the Holy Spirit moved all throughout the Old Testament times, and when He moved, supernatural power was always released. The same holds true during New Testament times.

The Holy Spirit Was Intimately Involved in Jesus' Life

A careful study of the gospels reveals that the Holy Spirit was involved in every aspect of Jesus' life. Think about the angel Gabriel's appearance and announcement to the Virgin Mary. "And, behold, thou shalt conceive in thy womb, and bring forth a son, and shalt call his name Jesus" (Luke 1:31).

Perplexed by the words that left the angel's lips, Mary asked respectfully, "…How shall this be, seeing I know not a man? And the angel answered and said unto her, The Holy Ghost shall come upon thee, and the power of the Highest shall overshadow thee: therefore also that holy thing which shall be born of thee shall be called the Son of God" (Luke 1:34,35).

Who was responsible for supernaturally conceiving Christ in Mary's womb? It was the work of the Holy Spirit. He moved upon Mary, and the miraculous took place. When the Holy Spirit moves, new life is conceived. Just like Mary, when we submit to the plans of God and allow His Spirit to move in our lives, we become impregnated with new life.

Flash forward 30 years, and we come to a milestone in Jesus' life that would effectively launch Him into full-time ministry. After He carefully made His way through the murky water, Jesus submissively stood before John the Baptist to be baptized. The Bible says, "And Jesus, when he was baptized, went up straightway out of the water: and, lo, the heavens were opened unto him, and he saw the Spirit of God descending like a dove, and lighting upon him" (Matthew 3:16).

Here again, we see the divine movement of the Holy Spirit — He descended gently on Jesus like a dove. In that moment, the Lord was baptized in the Holy Spirit and supernaturally energized for His ministry. In fact, Jesus was so full of the Holy Spirit, John declared, "…God's Spirit is upon him without measure or limit" (John 3:34 *TLB*).

Clearly, the Holy Spirit had free rein in the life of Christ, and He was actively involved in every aspect of His existence from His conception to His resurrection.

The Book of Acts Is a Portfolio of the Holy Spirit in Action

Just after the four gospels is the book of Acts, and while it is definitely a book of Early Church history, it is also a *pattern book* that set the precedent for the Church throughout all the ages. Again and again, it shows us that when the Holy Spirit is allowed to move freely, the miraculous always manifests. The apostles and people in the Early Church had hearts that were open to the Holy Spirit moving, and He never disappointed.

The Holy Spirit Moved on the Day of Pentecost

Just before ascending into Heaven to take His seat at the right hand of God the Father, Jesus told His faithful followers, "But ye shall receive power, after that the Holy Ghost is come upon you: and ye shall be witnesses unto me both in Jerusalem, and in all Judaea, and in Samaria, and unto the uttermost part of the earth" (Acts 1:8). When the Spirit moved on the people on the Day of Pentecost, they received *power*.

In Greek, the word "power" is *dunamis*, which is the New Testament word for *explosive power*. This word is used to describe *the full might of an advancing army* as well as *the force of nature displayed in a tornado or hurricane.*

Thus, when Jesus told them that they would receive power when the Spirit came upon them, He was saying, "When you allow the Holy Spirit to move in your life, you will become like *a force of nature* to be reckoned with. God's power will flow through you *like an advancing army* to drive back darkness and to take new territory."

Sure enough, as the disciples waited and prayed in the upper room, the Bible says, "…They were all filled with the Holy Ghost, and began to speak with other tongues, as the Spirit gave them utterance" (Acts 2:4). Because they were open to and desirous of the Holy Spirit moving, they received the gifts of the Spirit and the fire of God in the Church. These are the things we too can expect when we allow the Holy Spirit to move.

The Holy Spirit Moved When the Disciples Prayed

In Acts 3, we find Peter and John heading to the temple for the scheduled hour of prayer, and along the way they met a lame man at the Beautiful Gate. Upon seeing him, they perceived a prime opportunity to allow the Holy Spirit to move in the man's situation. With a fearless boldness, Peter declared, "…In the name of Jesus Christ of Nazareth rise up and walk" (Acts 3:6). The Bible says, "…Immediately his feet and ankle bones received strength. And he leaping up stood, and walked, and entered with them into the temple, walking, and leaping, and praising God" (Acts 3:7,8). This is a picture of the Holy Spirit in action.

Every time the First Century believers welcomed the Holy Spirit into their situations, He moved mightily. That's what we see taking place in the Upper Room when the disciples were seeking the Lord for strength. Acts 4:31 says, "And when they had prayed, the place was shaken where they were assembled together; and they were all filled with the Holy Ghost, and they spake the word of God with boldness." Just imagine! The building where you are praying begins to physically shake by the power of the Holy Spirit!

The Holy Spirit Released Healing Through Peter's Shadow

Events like these were a common occurrence in the Early Church. When the Holy Spirit was allowed to move, He seized the opportunity and performed many signs and wonders through the hands of the apostles. According to Scripture, the result was that "believers were the more added to the Lord, multitudes both of men and women" (Acts 5:14).

One of the most mindboggling series of miracles to be noted in Scripture is found in Acts 5:15 and 16. Here it is reported that the Holy Spirit was moving so mightily, "…That they brought forth the sick into the streets, and laid them on beds and couches, that at the least the shadow of Peter passing by might overshadow some of them. There came also a multitude out of the cities round about unto Jerusalem, bringing sick folks, and them which were vexed with unclean spirits: and they were healed every one."

This passage is an example of what happens when we remove the restrictions off the Holy Spirit. These people were thinking outside the religious box, discarding every preconceived notion of how the Spirit would and wouldn't operate. These people were so desirous to see the Holy Spirit move, they placed sick people in Peter's shadow believing they would be healed — and they were!

The Disciples Displayed the Dynamic Power of the Holy Spirit

Again and again, when the people of God gave opportunity for the Holy Spirit to move, He moved. Acts 6:8 says, "And Stephen, full of faith and power, did great wonders and miracles among the people." What is interesting about Stephen is that he wasn't an apostle, a prophet, or a pastor. He was what we would call an ordinary layman in the Church responsible for the daily distribution of food to widows and those in need. Yet through this ordinary man, the Holy Spirit did extraordinary things!

When we come to Acts 8, we see that the believers in Jerusalem were scattered as a result of persecution. Philip was one of the people who seized the opportunity to relocate. The Bible says, "Then Philip went down to the city of Samaria, and preached Christ unto them. And the people with one accord gave heed unto those things which Philip spake, hearing and seeing the miracles which he did. For unclean spirits, crying with loud voice, came out of many that were possessed with them: and many taken with palsies, and that were lame, were healed. And there was great joy in that city" (Acts 8:5-8).

The Holy Spirit Moved on Gentiles in the Same Way

Amazingly, in the midst of great difficulty, the Holy Spirit moved mightily among the Samaritans. Demons were cast out, crippled people were made whole, and healings of all kinds were on display. And just as the Holy Spirit moved then, He desires to move now. The miracles He manifested in others He wants to manifest in you.

Several years after the Day of Pentecost and the birth of the Church, the Holy Spirit began to move in a direction that He had never moved in before. Up until then, Jews were the primary audience for the Gospel. But in an unexpected turn of events, the Holy Spirit broke away from the norm and began ministering to Gentiles.

The Bible says, "While Peter yet spake these words [the Gospel], the Holy Ghost fell on all them which heard the word. And they of the circumcision which believed were astonished, as many as came with Peter, because that on the Gentiles also was poured out the gift of the Holy Ghost" (Acts 10:44,45). Clearly, seeing and hearing the Gentiles be filled with the Holy Spirit was a major turning point in the history of the Church.

The Holy Spirit Foretold the Future and Gave Divine Direction

When Jesus described the ministry of the Holy Spirit, one of the things He said the Spirit would do is show us things that are yet to come (*see* John 16:13). That is exactly what He did in Acts 11:28-30 when He moved on a certain prophet by the name of Agabus. Through Agabus, the Holy Spirit let believers know that a great famine was coming throughout the world, which actually did take place during the days of Claudius Caesar. Because believers were forewarned, they were able to prepare and send relief to fellow believers in Judea.

The Holy Spirit also granted vital direction to the leaders of the church in Antioch. The Bible says, "As they ministered to the Lord, and fasted, the Holy Ghost said, Separate me Barnabas and Saul for the work whereunto I have called them" (Acts 13:2). In this case, when the Spirit moved, Paul and Barnabas were divinely selected and launched into ministry to the Gentiles.

During their travels, they brought the Gospel to many dark, pagan cities in the Roman Empire — including the city of Lystra. It was there they encountered a man who had been crippled from birth and had never walked. The same Holy Spirit that launched Paul and Barnabas into ministry moved upon Paul to declare healing to this lame man. Acts 14:10 says, "[Paul] said with a loud voice, stand upright on thy feet. And he leaped and walked."

Again and again, the Holy Spirit moved through the apostle Paul to manifest the miraculous. This is seen all throughout the second half of the book of Acts, including the time when Paul returned to the great city of Ephesus and he ran into a group of men that had been disciples of John the Baptist. After sharing the message of the Gospel and leading these men to salvation in Christ, Paul laid his hands on them and "…the Holy Spirit came on them, and they spoke in tongues and prophesied" (Acts 19:6 *NIV*). Speaking in tongues and prophesying are two sure signs the Spirit is moving.

Before leaving Ephesus, the Bible says, "And God wrought special miracles by the hands of Paul: so that from his body were brought unto the sick handkerchiefs or aprons, and the diseases departed from them, and the evil spirits went out of them" (Acts 19:11-12).

Friend, happenings like these are interwoven throughout the pages of the Book of Acts. It is the *pattern book* that set the precedent for how the Holy Spirit is to move in the Church in every generation. His actions were not anomalies confined to the Early Church. They are meant for today — they are meant for you!

If we will remove all the restrictions from the Holy Spirit and allow Him to move freely, Jesus Christ's power will be released in our lives, our families, and in our churches. It is what will happen for you if you'll remove the restrictions and allow the Holy Spirit to move.

STUDY QUESTIONS

Study to shew thyself approved unto God, a workman that needeth not to be ashamed, rightly dividing the word of truth.
— 2 Timothy 2:15

1. The Bible says that Jesus was supernaturally conceived by the Holy Spirit. In what other ways was the Holy Spirit intimately involved in Jesus' life? Take a few moments to look up these passages for the answers.

   • Luke 1:35 — Jesus was *conceived* by the Holy Spirit.

- Acts 10:38; Isaiah 11:1-3 _____

  _____

- Matthew 4:1; Luke 4:1 _____

  _____

- Hebrews 9:14 _____

  _____

- Romans 8:11 _____

  _____

2. Through Agabus, the Holy Spirit let believers know that a great famine was coming throughout the world, and they were able to prepare for it (*see* Acts 11:28-30). What promise is demonstrated here that is available to you? (*See* Amos 3:7; John 16:13; First Corinthians 2:9,10.)

PRACTICAL APPLICATION

But be ye doers of the word, and not hearers only, deceiving your own selves.
—James 1:22

1. Can you remember a time when you surrendered yourself to God and allowed the Holy Spirit to move freely in your life? Describe what took place.

2. One reason we don't see more supernatural activity in the Church today is because we have restricted the movement of the Holy Spirit. How about you? Is there any area in your life that you have made "off limits" to the Holy Spirit? If so, where? If you don't know why you've restricted the Holy Spirit, ask Him to show you, and then give Him free access.

3. At the beginning of creation, the Holy Spirit moved across the formless void and darkness of the earth and brought order, structure, and meaning to it. Are there areas in your life that are empty and dark? Pray and invite the Holy Spirit to move in you and release His creative power that brings order, structure, and meaning to your life.

TOPIC

The Holy Spirit: Oil and Dew

SCRIPTURES

1. **Acts 10:38** — How God anointed Jesus of Nazareth with the Holy Ghost and with power: who went about doing good, and healing all that were oppressed of the devil; for God was with him.

2. **Genesis 28:18,19** — And Jacob rose up early in the morning, and took the stone that he had put for his pillows, and set it up for a pillar, and poured oil upon the top of it. And he called the name of that place Bethel....

3. **Exodus 30:22-31** — Moreover the Lord spake unto Moses, saying, Take thou also unto thee principal spices, of pure myrrh five hundred shekels, and of sweet cinnamon half so much, even two hundred and fifty shekels, and of sweet calamus two hundred and fifty shekels, and of cassia five hundred shekels, after the shekel of the sanctuary, and of oil olive an hin: and thou shalt make it an oil of holy ointment, an ointment compound after the art of the apothecary: it shall be an holy anointing oil. And thou shalt anoint the tabernacle of the congregation therewith, and the ark of the testimony, and the table and all his vessels, and the candlestick and his vessels, and the altar of incense, and the altar of burnt offering with all his vessels, and the laver and his foot. And thou shalt sanctify them, that they may be most holy: whatsoever toucheth them shall be holy. And thou shalt anoint Aaron and his sons, and consecrate them, that they may minister unto me in the priest's office. And thou shalt speak unto the children of Israel, saying, This shall be an holy anointing oil unto me throughout your generations.

4. **Luke 4:18,19** — The Spirit of the Lord is upon me, because he hath anointed me to preach the gospel to the poor; he hath sent me to heal the brokenhearted, to preach deliverance to the captives, and recovering of sight to the blind, to set at liberty them that are bruised, to preach the acceptable year of the Lord.

5. **2 Corinthians 1:21** — Now he which stablisheth us with you in Christ, and hath anointed us, is God.

6. **James 5:14-15** — Is any sick among you? let him call for the elders of the church; and let them pray over him, anointing him with oil in the name of the Lord: and the prayer of faith shall save the sick, and the Lord shall raise him up; and if he have committed sins, they shall be forgiven him.

7. **1 John 2:27** — But the anointing which ye have received of him abideth in you, and ye need not that any man teach you: but as the same anointing teacheth you of all things, and is truth, and is no lie, and even as it hath taught you, ye shall abide in him.

8. **Psalm 133:1-3** — Behold, how good and how pleasant it is for brethren to dwell together in unity! It is like the precious ointment upon the head, that ran down upon the beard, even Aaron's beard: that went down to the skirts of his garments; as the dew of Hermon, and as the dew that descended upon the mountains of Zion: for there the Lord commanded the blessing, even life for evermore.

GREEK WORDS

1. "anointed" — ἔχρισέν (*chrio*): to anoint with oil; a form of (*cheira*) means the human hand

SYNOPSIS

In our first lesson, we learned that when we remove all the restrictions from the Holy Spirit and allow Him to move freely, He causes miraculous things to take place. We see this principle throughout Scripture, beginning in Genesis 1:1 and 2. At the dawn of creation, the Holy Spirit was there, moving upon the chaos and confusion of the world, bringing divine order and structure. When the Holy Spirit moved, God's creative power was released. The same is true for you. If you will create an environment that invites the Spirit to move, His creative power will be released in *your* life.

The emphasis of this lesson:

The Holy Spirit is symbolized in Scripture in 15 primary ways. In this lesson, we will focus on what is meant by Him being depicted as oil and dew.

Throughout Scripture, there are 15 primary symbols, or metaphors, used to represent the Holy Spirit. They describe the person, the power, and the work of the Spirit.

The Holy Spirit is referred to as:

1. Oil
2. Dew
3. Rain
4. A River
5. Water or Living Water
6. Fire
7. A Dove
8. Clothing
9. Wind
10. The Gift
11. A Seal
12. The Earnest of our salvation
13. Glory
14. Light
15. Wine

All of these are symbols, emblems, or metaphors to describe the person, the power, and the work of the Holy Spirit.

Jesus Was Anointed With the Oil of the Spirit

In the Bible, the Holy Spirit is referred to as *oil* 200 times. This metaphor is seen repeatedly in both the Old and New Testaments. One of the most important verses depicting the Spirit as oil is in connection with the ministry of Jesus. Acts 10:38 says, "How God anointed Jesus of Nazareth with the Holy Ghost and with power: who went about doing good, and healing all that were oppressed of the devil; for God was with him."

The word "anointed" in this verse is from the Greek word *chrió*, which means *to anoint with oil*. Actually, the word *chrió* is a form of the Greek word for *the human hand* — the word *cheira*. This means that when a person was "anointed," someone usually put oil on their hands and then began to rub or massage the oil downward onto the person being anointed.

Therefore, when the Bible says God "anointed" Jesus with the Holy Spirit and Power, it literally means God put His hands on Jesus and imparted the anointing of His Holy Spirit into Him, just like when a person was anointed with oil. And when God imparted the anointing of the Spirit into Jesus' life, it came with God's mighty power. For God was with Him!

Oil Is Inseparably Linked to God's Presence

Interestingly, the very first time oil is seen as a symbol of the Holy Spirit is in the Old Testament. When Jacob — the son of Isaac and grandson of Abraham — was traveling, God appeared to him while he was sleeping and spoke to him, promising to bless him and to be with him always. How did Jacob respond? The Bible says, "And Jacob rose up early in the morning, and took the stone that he had put for his pillows, and set it up for a pillar, and poured *oil* upon the top of it. And he called the name of that place Bethel…" (Genesis 28:18,19).

The word "Bethel" means *house of God* or *the place where God lives*. Thus, the first mention of oil in Scripture is inseparably connected with the supernatural presence of God — the place where His Spirit lives. Jacob poured oil on the stone where he laid his head because oil represented the presence and power of God that He had encountered in that place.

Anointing Oil Was Applied to Everything in the Tabernacle

In Exodus 30, God spoke to Moses, instructing him on how to make the various furnishings of the tabernacle. In verses 22 through 28, He told Moses how to craft the anointing oil, which was to be used everywhere in the tabernacle. The Bible says:

> **"Moreover the Lord spake unto Moses, saying, Take thou also unto thee principal spices, of pure myrrh five hundred shekels, and of sweet cinnamon half so much, even two hundred and fifty shekels, and of sweet calamus two hundred and fifty shekels, and of cassia five hundred shekels, after the shekel of the sanctuary, and of oil olive an hin: and thou shalt make it an oil of holy ointment, an ointment compound after the art of the apothecary: it shall be an holy anointing oil" (Exodus 30:22-25).**

Again, the oil of holy ointment represented the presence and power of God's Holy Spirit. What was Moses to do with this oil? God said:

> **"And thou shalt anoint the tabernacle of the congregation therewith, and the ark of the testimony, and the table and all his vessels, and the candlestick and his vessels, and the altar of incense, and the altar of burnt offering with all his vessels, and the laver and his foot. (Exodus 30:26-28).**

This verse makes it emphatically clear that everything in the tabernacle was to be anointed with holy oil. Likewise, God wants us to anoint everything in our lives, in our homes, and in our churches with the oil of the Spirit. What else was the oil to provide? God said:

> **"And thou shalt sanctify them, that they may be most holy: whatsoever toucheth them shall be holy. And thou shalt anoint Aaron and his sons, and consecrate them, that they may minister unto me in the priest's office. And thou shalt speak unto the children of Israel, saying, This shall be an holy anointing oil unto me throughout your generations" (Exodus 30:29-31).**

The oil of the Holy Spirit touches us and comes into our lives the moment we get saved. Through these verses, God is telling us that when the oil of the Holy Spirit comes into our lives, it sanctifies us, consecrates us, and it sets us apart for His use for the rest of our lives. We need the oil of the Holy Spirit — the anointing — to bring the presence and power of God into our homes, our churches, and everywhere we go.

Eight Ways Oil Was Used That Defines the Ministry of the Holy Spirit

1. Consecration of Priests
(Exodus 30:30; Leviticus 4:3-5; Numbers 3:3)

When a priest was installed into the ministry he was always anointed with oil, because oil represents the Presence of the Holy Spirit.

2. Consecration of Kings
(1 Samuel 10:1; 15:17; 16:13; 2 Samuel 2:4,7; 5:3; 1 Kings 1:39)

Like priests, when a king was installed into office, he was anointed with oil, and that oil represented the presence of the Holy Spirit that consecrated him, sanctified him, it set him aside. The moment the oil was applied, it empowered the king with the anointing of the Holy Spirit for service.

3. The Messiah had the title "Anointed"

(Psalm 2:2)

The word "Messiah" means *The Anointed One*. There are examples of this throughout Scripture, but one of the most notable ones is Psalm 2:2, which refers to the "Messiah" as the Lord's anointed. Here, the word "Anointed" in the original language is capitalized, which means the Messiah was *more anointed* than anyone else. God put His Spirit upon the Messiah, who is Jesus. That is why the Holy Spirit moved upon Luke to write, "How God anointed Jesus of Nazareth with the Holy Ghost and with power…" (Acts 10:38). God put the Holy Spirit upon Jesus without measure (*see* John 3:34). That oil represents the presence and the power of the Holy Spirit.

4. Anointing of oil symbolizes the filling and empowering of the Holy Spirit

(1 Samuel 16:13; Zechariah 4:1-6; Matthew 25:1-13; Acts 1:8; Galatians 5:16; Ephesians 5:17,18)

Again and again, oil is used to symbolize the Holy Spirit, and where the oil is, there the presence and power of God live. When a person repents of sin and declares that Jesus is their Lord and Savior, that oil of the Holy Spirit enters their life and consecrates them, sanctifies them, and separates them for God's service for the rest of their life.

5. Jesus was "anointed" with the Holy Spirit

(Luke 4:18,19)

Even Jesus Himself used the concept of oil to describe the anointing of God that was upon Him. We see this exclusively in Luke's gospel, where Jesus stood up as a visiting rabbi and read from the ancient text of Isaiah 61. He declared, "The Spirit of the Lord is upon me, because he hath anointed me to preach the gospel to the poor; he hath sent me to heal the brokenhearted, to preach deliverance to the captives, and recovering of sight to the blind, to set at liberty them that are bruised, to preach the acceptable year of the Lord" (Luke 4:18,19).

In this passage, Jesus conveys His understanding of the anointing perfectly. He said, "The Spirit of the Lord is upon me, *because* He hath anointed Me...." The word "anointed" here means *to apply with a hand*. It was the equivalent of Jesus saying, "The Holy Spirit is upon Me because God has laid His hands on Me and placed the anointing of the Holy Spirit on Me." In the rest of the passage, Jesus described the results of the anointing: *to preach the Gospel to the poor; to heal the brokenhearted; to preach deliverance to the captives and recovering of sight to the blind; to set at liberty them that are bruised; and to preach the acceptable year of the Lord.* Thus, Jesus recognized that He'd been anointed with the oil of the Holy Spirit, and it is what empowered Him for ministry.

6. God anointed believers with the Holy Spirit
(2 Corinthians 1:21; 1 John 2:20,27)

God gives the oil of the Holy Spirit to every individual believer. Second Corinthians 1:21 says, "Now he which stablisheth us with you in Christ, and hath *anointed* us, is God." Hence, every person who repents of sin and makes Jesus the Lord of his life receives the Holy Spirit. And when the oil of the Spirit comes, He comes with His full presence and power to consecrate us, sanctify us, and separate us for God's purpose.

7. Anointing with oil symbolizes the healing work of the Holy Spirit
(James 5:14-15)

The oil of the Holy Spirit is also used symbolically to describe the healing power of God. We see this described in James 5:14 and 15, which says, "Is any sick among you? let him call for the elders of the church; and let them pray over him, *anointing him with oil* in the name of the Lord: and the prayer of faith shall save the sick, and the Lord shall raise him up; and if he have committed sins, they shall be forgiven him."

Praying for the sick was — and is — a divine moment when people release their faith. Although the oil itself has no magical healing powers, it is symbolic of the Holy Spirit's presence and power. In faith, the oil was (and is) applied, believing that God's healing power is available and present to make the sick person whole.

8. The oil symbolizes the teaching work of the Spirit
(1 John 2:27)

Lastly, the oil was used in Scripture to symbolize the teaching ministry of the Holy Spirit. We read about this in First John 2:27: "But the anointing which ye have received of him abideth in you, and ye need not that any man teach you: but as the same anointing teacheth you of all things, and is truth, and is no lie, and even as it hath taught you, ye shall abide in him."

This means once you are saved, the Holy Spirit moves into you, and He becomes your resident Teacher that permanently lives inside of you. In times when you don't have a human teacher available to you, you still have the anointing (oil) of the Holy Spirit teaching you and enabling you to know and understand things supernaturally by divine revelation.

So whenever you see oil mentioned in Scripture, you can know with certainty that it is symbolically referring to the Holy Spirit of God.

The Holy Spirit Is Also Symbolized by Dew

The second symbol of the Holy Spirit you need to be aware of is *dew*. One of the best scripture references for this is Psalm 133:1-3. Listen to what it says:

> **"Behold, how good and how pleasant it is for brethren to dwell together in unity! It is like the precious ointment upon the head, that ran down upon the beard, even Aaron's beard: that went down to the skirts of his garments; as the dew of Hermon, and as the dew that descended upon the mountains of Zion: for there the Lord commanded the blessing, even life for evermore."**

The word "dew" in this passage is talking about *the anointing of the Holy Spirit*. It is saying that the Holy Spirit in our lives is like "dew." To understand what this means, we have to understand what *dew* is and how it functions.

The fact of the matter is, moisture is in the air all the time, but you can't see or touch it. It's invisible. However, when the atmospheric conditions are just right, and the air cools down to the "dew point," the moisture in the air condenses and begins to manifest as water droplets all over everything. These droplets of water are what we call "dew." The "dew point" is the point at which the air molecules become fully saturated with moisture and cannot hold another drop. Suddenly, the moisture in the air appears everywhere — on outdoor furniture, plants, trees, grass, everything. The moisture was there all along. But it didn't manifest until the right conditions were met.

Psalm 133:3 says the anointing of the Spirit is much like dew. Verses 1 and 2 let us know that "unity" among God's people is the condition that causes the anointing to be released. In other words, "unity" is like the *dew point* that triggers the anointing to manifest. Like the moisture that is always in the air, the Holy Spirit is always with us. Although we may not see or sense His presence, He is there in our churches, our homes, and our lives. But He only manifests His presence where there is unity and peace.

When a church or person is in strife, they will most likely not experience the manifest presence of God. But when unity emerges, suddenly the power and presence of God begin to show up, and everyone gets touched by it. Evidence of the Spirit's anointing shows up everywhere. That is what happened when the disciples were unified in prayer on the Day of Pentecost. Indeed, where there is unity, "...the Lord commanded the blessing, even life for evermore" (Psalm 133:3).

In our next lesson, we are going to look at three more symbols of the Holy Spirit in Scripture: The Holy Spirit depicted as *rain*, *rivers*, and *Living Water*.

STUDY QUESTIONS

Study to shew thyself approved unto God, a workman that needeth not to be ashamed, rightly dividing the word of truth.
— 2 Timothy 2:15

1. In your own words, describe what it means to be *anointed*. After hearing the original meaning of the word "anointed" (the Greek word *chriō*), what fascinated you most? Why?

2. What scriptures are you most familiar with that talk about the oil (or anointing) of the Holy Spirit? Which one(s) means the most to you? Why?

3. Psalm 133 tells us that *unity* among God's people is the condition that causes the anointing of the Holy Spirit to be released in our lives. Where God sees unity, He commands His blessings (*see* verse 3). What are the instructions of Romans 12:16-18, and how are they connected with unity? (Consider Psalm 34:14; 1 Peter 3:11).

PRACTICAL APPLICATION

**But be ye doers of the word, and not hearers only,
deceiving your own selves.
— James 1:22**

1. Do you have a situation in which you are in desperate need for the Holy Spirit to move? Pray and ask God to show you how you can create an environment that invites His Spirit to move and release creative power in your life.

2. God told Moses to anoint the tabernacle and everything in it (*see* Exodus 30:26-28). According to First Corinthians 3:16 and 6:19 and Second Corinthians 6:16, *you* are the temple of the Holy Spirit. Pray and ask the Holy Spirit to release His anointing everywhere in your life, in your family, and in your home.

3. Be honest, how important has *unity* been in your life — with family members, church members, and coworkers? Is there anyone you know you're not in unity with right now? Take a moment and ask God to forgive you for being in strife and holding on to unforgiveness; then ask Him for strength to go and make things right with whoever you need to.

LESSON 3

TOPIC

The Holy Spirit: Rain, River, Water

SCRIPTURES

1. **Joel 2:23** — Be glad then, ye children of Zion, and rejoice in the Lord your God: for he hath given you the former rain moderately, and he will cause to come down for you the rain, the former rain, and the latter rain in the first month.

2. **Joel 2:28,29** — And it shall come to pass afterward, that I will pour out my spirit upon all flesh; and your sons and your daughters shall prophesy, your old men shall dream dreams, your young men shall see visions: and also upon the servants and upon the handmaids in those days will I pour out my spirit.

3. **John 7:37-39** — In the last day, that great day of the feast, Jesus stood and cried, saying, If any man thirst, let him come unto me, and drink. He that believeth on me, as the scripture hath said, out of his belly shall flow rivers of living water. (But this spake he of the Spirit, which they that believe on him should receive....)

4. **Psalm 46:4 (*NIV*)** — There is a river whose streams make glad the city of God....

5. **Isaiah 44:3 (*NIV*)** — For I will pour water on the thirsty land, and streams on the dry ground; I will pour out my Spirit on your offspring, and my blessing on your descendants.

6. **1 Corinthians 12:13** — For by one Spirit are we all baptized into one body, whether we be Jews or Gentiles, whether we be bond or free; and have been all made to drink into one Spirit.

GREEK WORDS

1. "flow" — ῥέω (*rheo*): pictures a rushing stream, so full that it overflows its banks

2. "living water" — ὕδατος ζῶντος (*hudatos zontos*): water that is living; water filled with vibrancy and life

3. "drink" — ποτίζω (*potidzo*): literally, to drink; consume; imbibe; irrigate

SYNOPSIS

In our last lesson, we learned about two symbols in Scripture that describe the ministry of the Holy Spirit. The first was *oil*, which appears about 200 times in the Old and New Testament. We also saw how the anointing of the Spirit is compared to the morning *dew*, which is seen in Psalm 133. Just as moisture is always in the air but is not visible until the conditions are right to meet the dew point, the presence and power of the Holy Spirit are always around us, but He will not manifest until we come together in unity. This is what is known as the corporate anointing. God promises that where there is unity, "...the Lord commanded the blessing, even life for evermore" (Psalm 133:3).

The emphasis of this lesson: Rain, River, and Water

In Scripture, the Holy Spirit is also often likened to *rain*, which reflects God's favor and presence; a *river*, which is teeming with life and brings great change; and *water*, which satisfies and refreshes our thirsty souls.

The Holy Spirit Is Like *Rain*

One of the most notable passages in the Bible where the Holy Spirit is paralleled with rain is in the book of Joel. The Scripture says, "Be glad then, ye children of Zion, and rejoice in the Lord your God: for he hath given you the former *rain* moderately, and he will cause to come down for you the *rain*, the *former rain*, and the *latter rain* in the first month" (Joel 2:23).

In Israel, rain was very important. Being an agrarian culture, everything in life centered around and depended on the two main rainy seasons. The *early rain* was the first rain, and it usually occurred during the months of October through November. This rain was vital as it softened the soil and facilitated the germination of the seeds that were planted and eventually grew in to crops. The *latter rain* was equally vital. It usually came between March and April, and it was essential for bringing the crops to full maturity so they could be harvested.

Moreover, rain in Scripture is associated with God's favor and His powerful presence. The right amount of rain was a blessing, bringing healthy crop growth and eventually a bountiful harvest. When the rain came at its proper time and in the proper amount, the people rejoiced. On the other hand, too much rain was destructive. It damaged fields and homes, destroyed crops, paralyzed life, and ruined the harvest. And a lack of rain was viewed by the people as God's displeasure. So having the right amount of rain at the right time was seen as God's favor.

Spiritually speaking, we need the right amount of rain at the right time in order for us to grow and for souls to be harvested. Just as the people of Israel were totally depended upon God to regulate the rain, as believers we are totally dependent on Him as well. Sometimes Christians who are not mature in the Lord will pray, "Oh Lord, let it rain, rain, rain, rain," not realizing that too much spiritual rain isn't good for us. God knows when we need rain and exactly how much to give us. We must learn to trust Him to give us the rain we need in due season.

The prophet Joel went on to say, "And it shall come to pass afterward, that I will pour out my spirit upon all flesh; and your sons and your daughters shall prophesy, your old men shall dream dreams, your young men shall see visions: and also upon the servants and upon the handmaids in those days will I pour out my spirit" (Joel 2:28,29). Metaphorically, God said through Joel, "I'm going to send an early rain upon the Church and a latter rain.

In the context of Scripture, rain symbolizes *the outpouring of the Holy Spirit*. The *early rain* — or outpouring — is what took place on the Day of Pentecost. The apostle Peter declared this in Acts 2. God brought the early rain of the Holy Spirit to prepare the soil of humanity to receive the seeds of the Gospel. With the early rain, God also forecasted that there will be a *latter rain*, or a latter outpouring of the Holy Spirit. The *latter rain* is essential to bring about the final harvest of souls just before the coming of Jesus. That is what we're experiencing today, and it will continue to increase as we come nearer to the rapture of the Church.

The Holy Spirit Is Like a *River*

Another strong emblem of the Holy Spirit in Scripture is the imagery of a *river*. Jesus most notably described this in John's gospel when He stood and cried "…If any man thirst, let him come unto me, and drink" (John 7:37). The word "drink" is the Greek word *potidzo*, which literally means *to drink deeply; consume*; or *imbibe*. It carries the idea of *being completely irrigated*. Thus, when Jesus said to come and "drink," He was saying, "If you're spiritually thirsty and hungry come to Me and drink deeply. I will completely irrigate every inch of your parched heart."

He went on to say, "He that believeth on me, as the scripture hath said, out of his belly shall flow rivers of living water. (But this spake he of the Spirit, which they that believe on him should receive…" (John 7:38,39).

Notice the phrase "out of his belly shall flow rivers of living water." The word "flow" in Greek is the word *rheo*, and it pictures *a mighty rushing stream that is so full it overflows its banks*. In this case, the stream is overflowing with "living water." This is a translation of the Greek words *hudatos zontos*, which describes *water that is living; water filled with vibrancy and life*. Here, Jesus Himself is comparing the refreshing, life-giving work of the Holy Spirit with a mighty rushing river that is teeming with life.

Rivers Bring Change. In addition to satisfying thirst and producing life, a river is also known for bringing *change*. Think of the mighty Mississippi River flowing through the center of the United States. The tremendous volume of water it carries is a powerful force that picks up things and moves them out of the way. In the same way, the Holy Spirit flowing in our lives picks things up — especially things that are outdated or no longer needed — and moves them out of the way.

When you pray for the "river of God" to move in your life, you're asking for the Holy Spirit to saturate your soul and spirit with His Living Water. And at the same time, you're giving Him permission to pick up and move things out of your life that are outdated, dead, or no longer needed.

Not only will God move unwanted things out of our life, but He will also move people out of His way that are resistant to what He is trying to accomplish. Again, the river of God is a powerful force that cannot be stopped. If anyone stands in opposition to Him, they will be removed. Indeed, the Holy Spirit is a mighty agent of change!

Rivers Vary in Size and Depth. It should also be noted that not all rivers are the same. For example, some rivers are very shallow, and because they lack depth they are noisy. In fact, the shallower the river, the noisier it is as it flows. Deep rivers, on the other hand, are much quieter as they make their way downstream. Some rivers are so deep they are nearly silent as they flow. And the deeper they are the more power they pack.

Similarly, there are some believers who are shallow and have a minimal flow of the Holy Spirit in their life. These shallow, immature Christians seem to make a lot of "noise" as they carry out their lives. Then there are other believers who are deep and have an enormous volume of the Holy Spirit flowing in and through their lives. These older, more mature Christians are virtually silent as they serve the Lord, but they pack the power of the Holy Spirit to effectively move things out of the way.

Rivers Separate into Different Streams. Many rivers start off as a single waterway and then separate into several streams as they meander along. One of the greatest factors determining the different branches is the lay of the land through which the river flows.

Likewise, there are different streams of how the Holy Spirit moves and manifests in the Church. The Bible confirms this, declaring, "There is a river whose streams make glad the city of God…" (Psalm 46:4 (*NIV*).

Here we see there is *one* river with *multiple* streams. Clearly, the Holy Spirit is one river that moves in countless ways. Just when you think He's going to move one way, He moves in a way that is totally unexpected. We need to be careful not to get stuck in doing things for God the same way. We need to be flexible and go with the flow of the Spirit.

The bottom line is, the Holy Spirit wants to move like a mighty river in your life. He wants you to jump in and surrender your life to His flow. Are you ready? The adventure awaits!

The Holy Spirit Is Like *Water*

In addition to being described as a *river* and as *rain*, the Bible also compares the ministry of the Holy Spirit to *water* itself. In Isaiah 44:3 (*NIV*), God said, "For I will pour water on the thirsty land and streams on the dry ground; I will pour out my Spirit on your offspring, and my blessing on your descendants."

In this verse, the second part clarifies the meaning of the first. God said He is going to pour out His Spirit like water on the thirsty ground — the ground being the offspring or descendants of His people. The apostle Paul also used the metaphor of *water* in First Corinthians 12:13 when he said, "For by one Spirit are we all baptized into one body, whether we be Jews or Gentiles, whether we be bond or free; and have been all made to *drink* into one Spirit."

Notice he said we "have been all made to drink into one Spirit." The word "drink" here is the Greek word *potidzo*, which means *to drink, to consume*, or *to be irrigated*. The use of this word tells us that God has created us in such a way that we can *drink* of the Holy Spirit. Hence, when we are spiritually thirsty for more of the Holy Spirit, God promises to satisfy our thirst by pouring out His Spirit!

What is interesting is that there is desert land in Israel today — land that has shown no signs of life for centuries — that is now blossoming with vegetation because engineers have developed specialized irrigation to water the land. That's what happens for us when the Holy Spirit begins to move in our lives. He irrigates us so wonderfully that the areas of our life that were once arid and fruitless now begin to produce abundant fruit!

Friend, the Holy Spirit is simply amazing! He works in our lives like *water*, like *rain*, and like a *river*. Indeed, He is a mighty hydrating force that refreshes, renews, and irrigates our souls to be wellsprings of vibrant life!

In our next lesson, we will return to the Scriptures and explore three more characteristics of the Holy Spirit, including the symbols of *fire*, a *dove*, and *clothing*.

STUDY QUESTIONS

Study to shew thyself approved unto God, a workman that needeth not to be ashamed, rightly dividing the word of truth.
— 2 Timothy 2:15

1. Jesus is the exact image of the Father (*see* Hebrews 1:3), and He longs to be in a close, vibrant relationship with you every day! In John 7:37, He said, "…If any man thirst, let him come unto me, and drink." He offers you another invitation in Matthew 11:28-30. What is this offer to "drink," and have you accepted this extraordinary opportunity?

2. Being refreshed by the water of the Spirit is something we need regularly — especially in the times in which we are living. According to First Corinthians 14:4, what is one of the best ways to tap into the river of living water inside you? What can you expect to happen every time you utilize this special gift from God? (*See* Romans 8:26,27.)

PRACTICAL APPLICATION

But be ye doers of the word, and not hearers only, deceiving your own selves.
— James 1:22

1. Spiritually speaking, we need the right amount of rain at the right time in order for us to grow and for souls to be harvested. Why do you think too much spiritual rain isn't good for us?

2. How would you describe the "river" of the Holy Spirit in your life? Would you say it is *deep*? *Shallow*? Or somewhere in between? What evidence can you point to that verifies your answer?

3. Does your relationship with God feel dry? Are you spiritually dehydrated? When was the last time you took a drink — a real deep drink — of the Living Water? If you need an adequate amount of water every day to function physically, don't you think you need the water of

the Holy Spirit to function spiritually? What changes can you make in your daily routine to take in more Living Water?

TOPIC

The Holy Spirit: Fire, Dove, and Clothing

SCRIPTURES

1. **Matthew 3:11** — I indeed baptize you with water unto repentance: but he that cometh after me is mightier than I, whose shoes I am not worthy to bear: he shall baptize you with the Holy Ghost, and with fire.

2. Acts 2:1-4 — And when the day of Pentecost was fully come, they were all with one accord in one place. And suddenly there came a sound from heaven as of a rushing mighty wind, and it filled all the house where they were sitting. And there appeared unto them cloven tongues like as of fire, and it sat upon each of them. And they were all filled with the Holy Ghost, and began to speak with other tongues, as the Spirit gave them utterance.

3. **Matthew 3:16** — And Jesus, when he was baptized, went up straightway out of the water: and, lo, the heavens were opened unto him, and he saw the Spirit of God descending like a dove, and lighting upon him.

4. **Luke 24:49** — And, behold, I send the promise of my Father upon you: but tarry ye in the city of Jerusalem, until ye be endued with power from on high.

5. **Acts 1:8** — But ye shall receive power, after that the Holy Ghost is come upon you: and ye shall be witnesses unto me both in Jerusalem, and in all Judaea, and in Samaria, and unto the uttermost part of the earth.

GREEK WORDS

1. "endued" — ἐνδύω (*enduo*): to be clothed; to sink into a garment; to array, clothe, endue, or to put on
2. "lo" — ἰδοὺ (*idou*): expresses shock, bewilderment, wonder and amazement
3. "behold" — ἰδοὺ (*idou*): expresses shock, bewilderment, wonder and amazement
4. "power" — δύναμις (*dunamis*): explosive, superhuman power with enormous energy that produces phenomenal, extraordinary, and unparalleled results; pictures the force of an entire army

SYNOPSIS

So far in our study of the symbols of the Holy Spirit, we have seen that the Bible metaphorically depicts the Spirit as *oil*, *dew*, *rain*, *a river*, and *water*.

Every believer receives the *oil* of the Holy Spirit the moment he or she is saved. This is the *anointing* of God that belongs to every believer. Second, the Holy Spirit functions as *dew* in our lives. Just as moisture is in the air at all times but only becomes visible under certain circumstances, the Holy Spirit is always with us, but He only manifests His presence when believers come together in unity (*see* Psalm 133:1-3).

Third, we saw that the Holy Spirit is like *rain*. God pours His Spirit out on us like the early rain and latter rain that fell on the land of Israel. He knows exactly how much rain of the Spirit we need at any given time, and He will send it to us if we will humble ourselves and pray for it. That is our part.

The Holy Spirit is also like a *river*. Jesus described this in John 7:38 when He said, "He that believeth on me, as the scripture hath said, out of his belly shall flow *rivers* of living water…." The Holy Spirit is like a mighty river filled with vibrancy, bringing us life and removing things that are hindering what He wants to do. His intention is to move like a river through the Church and flood us with His divine life.

The fifth symbol of the Holy Spirit we've studied is *water*. In Isaiah 44:3 (*NIV*), God said, "I will pour *water* upon the thirsty land and streams on the dry ground; I will pour out my *Spirit* on your offspring, and my blessing on your descendants." As Christians, God has fashioned us to "drink" of the Holy Spirit (*see* 1 Corinthians 12:13). He wants to flood us with His Spirit in such a way that we are completely irrigated and are able to produce abundant fruit.

The emphasis of this lesson:

The Bible depicts the Holy Spirit as *fire* that illuminates, warms, and energizes us. He's also represented as a *dove* that is gentle and peaceful when He works with us. Moreover, He is described as *clothing* that dresses us in His dynamic power.

The Holy Spirit Is a *Fire*

There are many beautiful church buildings throughout the world with remarkable architecture, stunning stonework, exquisite stained glass, and magnificent steeples. But these buildings lack what is most important — the *fire* of the Holy Spirit. It is the divine fire of the Spirit that sets us apart and sets us ablaze for God's glory.

John the Baptist — the forerunner who prepared the way for Jesus' ministry — said, "I indeed baptize you with water unto repentance: but he that cometh after me is mightier than I, whose shoes I am not worthy to bear: he shall baptize you with the Holy Ghost, and with *fire*" (Matthew 3:11).

What John prophesied is what began in the Upper Room over 2,000 years ago. The Bible says, "And when the day of Pentecost was fully come, they were all with one accord in one place. And suddenly there came a sound from heaven as of a rushing mighty wind, and it filled all the house where they were sitting. And there appeared unto them cloven tongues like as of *fire*, and it sat upon each of them. And they were all filled with the Holy Ghost, and began to speak with other tongues, as the Spirit gave them utterance" (Acts 2:1-4). When the Holy Spirit came, He came with fire.

Think about fire. It is vital to our very existence. It provides heat, generates energy, and illuminates the dark. It is needed for cooking, baking, and purifying. It empowers engines, drives ships and trains, and runs all types of machinery. What would life be like without fire? Our world would be a very cold, dark, primitive place. In many ways, life on earth would be like trying to live on the surface of the moon.

In the same way, without the fire of the Holy Spirit, life would be a very cold, dark place spiritually. The Spirit provides us with warmth, illumination, and divine energy to function. The fire of the Holy Spirit incinerates what is not of God in our character and ignites that which is of Him.

Samuel Chadwick — a Wesleyan minister and author born in the mid-to-late 1800s — once wrote, "Spirit-filled souls are ablaze for God. They love with a love that glows. They serve with a faith that kindles. They serve with a devotion that consumes. They hate sin with fierceness that burns. They rejoice with a joy that radiates. Love is perfected in the fire of God." Friend, we have to have the fire of the Holy Spirit for survival, revival, and spiritual growth. It is not optional.

The Holy Spirit Is Like a *Dove*

In addition to being a fire, the Bible states that the Holy Spirit is like a *dove*. This symbol is seen most clearly at Jesus' baptism in the Jordan River. What is interesting about this milestone in Jesus' life is that it is recorded in all four gospels. Looking at Matthew's account, the Scripture says, "And Jesus, when he was baptized, went up straightway out of the water: and, lo, the heavens were opened unto him, and he saw the Spirit of God descending like a dove, and lighting upon him" (Matthew 3:16). You will also find this in Mark 1:10; Luke 3:22; and John 1:32.

Notice the word "lo" in this verse. It is the Greek term *idou*, which expresses *shock, bewilderment, wonder* and *amazement*. It is the equivalent of Matthew saying, "Wow! Can you imagine it! What I'm about to tell you is so absolutely amazing it leaves me speechless." Essentially, Matthew was inserting his own commentary about his gospel account.

He said the Holy Spirit descended on Jesus *like* a dove. He didn't say the Spirit is a dove. Clearly, the Holy Spirit is not a bird with feathers that flies around. He is the third person of the Trinity who is fully God, and at times He exhibits the characteristics of a dove. This means the Holy Spirit is gentle like a dove. Very often when He comes to work in our lives, He is tender and loving in the way He speaks to us and corrects us. His methods are calm and soothing like that of a dove.

It is also important to note that a dove will not just land and rest anywhere. The place he alights must be peaceful, and he must feel safe. In the same way, the Holy Spirit is most drawn to us when we are living in peace. When He rests on us, He brings the peaceful presence of God and empowers us to live like Jesus. The Holy Spirit's dovelike qualities are certainly a treasured gift to us.

The Holy Spirit Covers Us Like *Clothing*

Another important symbol of the Holy Spirit found in Scripture is *clothing*. Just before ascending into Heaven, Jesus spoke to His disciples about the ministry of the Holy Spirit and said, "And, behold, I send the promise of my Father upon you: but tarry ye in the city of Jerusalem, until ye be endued with power from on high" (Luke 24:49).

Note that Jesus began His statement with the word "Behold." Again, this is the Greek word *idou*, which denotes *bewilderment, shock, amazement, and wonder*. A better translation of this would be, "Wow! What I'm about to tell you is so amazing it is simply breathtaking!" Then Jesus proceeded to describe to tell them how the Holy Spirit would come.

He said, "...I send the promise of my Father *upon* you..." (Luke 24:49). The word "upon" is important. It is the exact same word used in Acts 1:8 when Jesus said, "But ye shall receive power, after that the Holy Ghost is come *upon* you...."

When Jesus spoke these words, the Holy Spirit was already living *in* the disciples. He had entered their lives the moment they were saved, which is recorded in John's gospel. Immediately after Jesus had been raised from the grave, He appeared to His disciples when they were shut up inside the Upper Room. After revealing His nail-scarred hands and his pierced side, the Bible says, "...He breathed on them, and saith unto them, Receive ye the Holy Ghost" (John 20:22). It was in that moment the disciples were born again.

But there was another experience with the Holy Spirit Jesus knew His disciples needed. That is why He told them, "...Tarry ye in the city of Jerusalem, until ye be endued with power from on high" (Luke 24:49). The word "endued" in this verse is the Greek word *enduo*, which means *to be clothed; to array, clothe, endue, or to put on*. This word carries the idea of *sinking into a garment*; it depicts *one who is so comfortable in his clothing, he sinks into it*.

Essentially, what Jesus is telling us is that the Holy Spirit *clothes* us with His power, and we are to become so comfortable in His power that we sink right into it — like a familiar environment in which we live. The power of the Holy Spirit is to be every believer's new surroundings.

This brings us to the word "power" found in Luke 24:49 and Acts 1:8. Jesus told the disciples the Holy Spirit would come upon them and they would be clothed with and receive "power." This is the Greek word *dunamis,* and it describes *explosive, superhuman power with enormous energy that produces phenomenal, extraordinary, and unparalleled results.* It is the same word used to denote *the full force of an entire advancing army.* It's also the Greek word used to describe *a force of nature like a hurricane, a tornado, or an earthquake.*

This means when the power of the Holy Spirit comes upon us, we become like *a supernatural force of nature.* God's power is unleashed through us to produce *phenomenal, extraordinary, unparalleled results.* Like a mighty, advancing army, His divine strength enables us to march forward, push back the forces of darkness, and take new territory. That is what happens when we are baptized in the *dunamis* power of the Holy Spirit.

In our next lesson, we will focus on the Holy Spirit being depicted as a rushing, mighty *wind.*

STUDY QUESTIONS

Study to shew thyself approved unto God, a workman that needeth not to be ashamed, rightly dividing the word of truth.
— 2 Timothy 2:15

1. What would your life be like *without* the fire of the Holy Spirit? Has His fire gone out in you? Carefully read, heed, and put into practice Paul's instruction to young Timothy who dealt with the same dilemma (*see* 1 Timothy 4:14 and 2 Timothy 1:6).

2. Hebrews 12:29 declares, "For our God is a consuming fire." One of the qualities of His fire in our lives is depicted in First Corinthians 3:13-15; First Peter 1:6,7; and Malachi 3:2-4. What is this necessary quality?

3. Are you spiritually exhausted? Do you feel mentally, emotionally, and physically depleted? God stands ready, willing, and *more than able* to release His tangible, supernatural energy into you! Take a few moments to reflect on His words in Isaiah 40:28-31. What is He

speaking to you through this passage? How can you take this promise and make it a personal prayer for God's strength?

PRACTICAL APPLICATION

**But be ye doers of the word, and not hearers only,
deceiving your own selves.
— James 1:22**

1. One of the ways the Holy Spirit operates in our lives is like a *dove*. Can you recall a time when the Holy Spirit handled you with *dove-like* qualities? What do you appreciate most about this aspect of His nature?

2. Like the disciples in the Early Church, Jesus wants you to be "endued" with the power of the Holy Spirit. That is, He wants you to be *clothed* with His supernatural might so comfortably that you sink right into it. How comfortable are you with the power of the Holy Spirit? Is there anything specific that makes you feel uncomfortable with Him? If so, what is it?

3. Are you experiencing spiritual coldness in your life? Are things dark and dull? Are you lacking spiritual energy? Take time now to pray and ask the Holy Spirit to impart fresh fire in your life. Ask Him to illuminate the truth about God and His Word that you need to see in this season.

LESSON 5

TOPIC

The Holy Spirit: Wind

SCRIPTURES

1. **John 3:8** — The wind bloweth where it listeth, and thou hearest the sound thereof, but canst not tell whence it cometh, and whither it goeth: so is every one that is born of the Spirit.

2. **Acts 2:2** — And suddenly there came a sound from heaven as of a rushing mighty wind, and it filled all the house where they were sitting.

GREEK WORDS

1. "wind" — **πνεῦμα** (*pneuma*): spirit, breath, wind; a reference to the Holy Spirit moving as wind

2. "bloweth" — **πνέω** (*pneo*): to blow as wind would blow; you cannot see it, but you can feel its effects

3. "listeth" — **θέλει** (*thelei*): literally, He wishes; to will, wish, desire, intend, design

4. "hearest" — **ἀκούω** (*akouo*): hear; comprehend; perceive; where we get the word "acoustics"

5. "sound" — **φωνή** (*phone*): sound; noise; cry; voice

6. "Spirit" — **Πνεύματος** (*Pneumatos*): the Spirit, referring to the Holy Spirit

7. "suddenly" — **ἄφνω** (*aphno*): pictures something that took them off guard and by surprise

8. "there came" — **ἐγένετο** (*egeneto*): a form of **γίνομαι** (*ginomai*); something that happens unexpectedly or that catches one off guard

9. "sound" — **ἦχος** (*echos*): used also in Luke 21:5 to describe the deafening roar of the sea

10. "rushing" — **φερομένης** (*pheromenes*): the present-passive participle of **φέρω** (*phero*), which means to be carried, borne, or driven, and it agrees with the idea of something borne or driven downward very loudly

11. "mighty" — **βιαίας** (*biaias*): violent; this sound thundered like the roaring of a sea or a mighty wind that swept downward very loudly and violently

12. "wind" — **πνοή** (*pnoe*): wind so loud that one may be tempted to cover his ears from the overpowering noise of it

SYNOPSIS

From the very first mention of the Holy Spirit in Scripture, we see that when He is present, supernatural activity is taking place. Metaphorically, the Spirit is depicted as 15 primary symbols.

The Holy Spirit is like…

- The anointing *oil* that heals, strengthens, and teaches us.

- The *dew* of heaven that touches everyone when there is unity among God's people.
- The early and latter *rain* that prepares the soil to receive seed and produce a bumper harvest.
- A mighty *river* flowing and teeming with life.
- *Water* that saturates and satisfies the thirsty souls of mankind.
- A *fire* that illuminates, energizes, and purifies.
- A *dove* that is tender and gentle in His dealings.
- *Clothing* that dresses us in dynamic, supernatural power.

Indeed, there is no one equal to the extraordinary Holy Spirit of God!

The emphasis of this lesson:

The Holy Spirit is like a rushing mighty wind; we cannot see Him, but we can certainly feel the effects of His presence. He removes pollutants and dispels the stink of stagnation from our lives. We need the wind of the Holy Spirit to experience the supernatural in our lives.

Wind Is a Powerful Force

Growing up in the state of Oklahoma, Rick and Denise Renner personally experienced the powerful effects of wind. Tornadoes are a regular occurrence in the Sooner state, which averages 52 twisters a year, but was hit with a whopping 146 cyclones in 2019. Extremely low hanging clouds glowing with an eerie greenish tint is a sure sign that ferocious winds are just about to blow.

What is interesting is that oftentimes, just before a funnel cloud forms and touches down, a strange lull will blanket the area. Birds will grow quiet, trees will settle in stillness, and the wind will come to a standstill. Then suddenly, out of nowhere, a twister will emerge with winds ranging from 100mph to more than 250mph, delivering catastrophic destruction to whatever is in its path.

Without question, wind is a powerful force of nature, and while it can be extremely destructive, it also brings us many positive benefits. Think about the early explorers who sailed the high seas to establish new trade routes and discover new lands. It wasn't gas engines or nuclear propulsion that got them where they needed to go — it was *wind*. People like Christopher

Columbus and the Pilgrims were transported across the waters by wind power.

Wind drives machines, powers turbine engines, and sets windmills in motion to create energy and manufacture all types of goods. What's more, wind removes pollution and stagnation, bringing refreshing, oxygenated air that we need to breathe. The fact is, without wind, we wouldn't have the civilization we have today.

In Scripture, the Holy Spirit is likened to the *wind* — wind that is essential for life. Spiritually, He removes pollutants and dispels the stink of stagnation from our lives. He invigorates our airways with refreshing, oxygenated air that energizes us to fulfill God's purpose in the earth. What would life be like without the wind of the Spirit?

Jesus Compared the Work of the Spirit to the Blowing of the Wind

In an evening conversation with a Pharisee named Nicodemus, Jesus talked about the Kingdom of God and how we can only enter it by being born of the Spirit. He then compared the work of the Holy Spirit to the wind, saying, "The wind bloweth where it listeth, and thou hearest the sound thereof, but canst not tell whence it cometh, and whither it goeth: so is every one that is born of the Spirit" (John 3:8).

The word "wind" here is the Greek word *pneuma*, which means *spirit, breath, wind*; it is a direct reference to the Holy Spirit moving as wind. The word "bloweth" in Greek is *pneo*, and it means *to blow as wind would blow; you cannot see it, but you can feel its effects*. When the Holy Spirit ministers to us, He is just like the wind; we cannot see Him, but we can certainly feel the effects of His presence.

Jesus went on to say that the Holy Spirit "bloweth where it listeth." In Greek, "listeth" is the word *thelei*, which literally means *He wishes*. It carries the idea *to will, wish, desire, intend, or design*. Although we can't see the Spirit, Jesus said we can "hearest the sound thereof." The word "hearest" is the Greek term *akouo*, which means *hear, comprehend*, or *perceive*. It is from where we get the word "acoustics." When the Holy Spirit moves, you can hear and comprehend the "sound." This word "sound" is very important. It is the Greek word *phone*, and it describes a *sound; noise; cry*; or *voice*. The inclusion of this word tells us that when the Holy Spirit moves, He can be very loud — just like the howling of tornadic winds.

Continuing His description of the ministry of the Holy Spirit, Jesus told Nicodemus — *and us* — that we "…canst not tell whence it cometh, and whither it goeth: so is every one that is born of the Spirit" (John 3:8). The word "Spirit" is the Greek word *Pneumatos*, and it is capitalized here, which means it is referring to *the Holy Spirit*. Thus, Jesus Himself likened the work of the Holy Spirit to the wind.

The Holy Spirit Arrived on the Day of Pentecost Like a 'Rushing, Mighty Wind'

Like Jesus, Luke also used the imagery of wind to describe the movement of the Holy Spirit on the Day of Pentecost. In Acts 2:2, he wrote, "And suddenly there came a sound from heaven as of a rushing mighty wind, and it filled all the house where they were sitting."

One of the first words Luke inserts is "suddenly" — the Greek word *aphno*, which pictures *something that took them off guard and by surprise*. To this, he added the phrase "there came," which is the Greek word *egeneto*, a form of the *ginomai*, which describes *something that happens unexpectedly or that catches one off guard*. On the Day of Pentecost, something suddenly and unexpectedly took place that totally caught the disciples off guard.

The Bible says, "And suddenly there came a sound from heaven…" (Acts 2:2). The word "sound" here is the Greek word *echos*. It is the same word used in Luke 21:5 to describe *the deafening roar of the sea*. If you have ever been caught in the middle of a storm, you know how loud it can be. It can be so deafening that you have to yell to the person next to you so they can hear what you're trying to say. That is the intensity of the noise being described by the Greek word *echos* — translated here as "sound." This means when the Holy Spirit came into the room on the Day of Pentecost, it was so loud it was nearly deafening. It is likely that the disciples began covering their ears to muffle the sound they were hearing.

In this case, the deafening sound they heard was that of "a rushing mighty wind." In Greek, the word "rushing" is *pheromones*, and it is the present-passive participle of *phero*, which means *to be carried, borne, or driven*. It agrees with the idea of *something borne or driven downward very loudly*.

The roaring sound in the Upper Room on the Day of Pentecost was being carried or driven by "mighty wind."

The word "mighty" in Greek is *biaias*, which describes *something violent*. This sound thundered like the roaring of a sea or a mighty wind that swept downward very loudly and violently. In Greek, the word for "wind" is *pnoe*, which describes *a wind so loud that one may be tempted to cover his ears from the overpowering noise of it*.

The use and arrangement of all these words lets us know that the Holy Spirit's arrival on the Day of Pentecost was no quiet event. It was *a boisterous, violent-sounding affair*. And while it wasn't destructive in nature, it was certainly a supercharged empowerment of the Spirit that energized the disciples to move forward and begin preaching the Gospel.

We Are Totally Dependent on the Wind of the Spirit

Friend, we need to have the *wind* of the Holy Spirit to experience the supernatural in our lives. When God formed Adam on the sixth day of creation, He was the perfect specimen of humanity. Every atom of his anatomy was flawlessly arranged and ordered. However, until God breathed into Adam's nostrils the breath of life (*see* Genesis 2:7), he was a lifeless corpse. It was, and still is, the wind of the Spirit that animates and energizes man.

In the same way, we can have perfect-looking lives, churches, businesses, and families and be doing all the right things that need to be done. But without the life-giving wind of the Holy Spirit breathing on us and on what we're doing, we're not going to accomplish anything. We need the wind of the Spirit to give us new life, fresh energy, and divine movement. We are totally dependent upon Him.

When the wind of the Spirit begins to blow, things begin to change. If you sense Him blowing in your life, don't resist Him. Raise your spiritual sails, catch His wind, and allow Him to take you to where He wants you to be. If you let Him, He will reenergize you with the same Spirit that raised Christ from the dead (*see* Romans 8:11).

In the coming lessons, we're going to see how the Holy Spirit is also symbolized as a *gift*, a *seal, the earnest of our salvation*, *glory*, *light*, and *wine*.

STUDY QUESTIONS

**Study to shew thyself approved unto God, a workman that needeth
not to be ashamed, rightly dividing the word of truth.
— 2 Timothy 2:15**

1. What new insights did you learn about the Holy Spirit operating like *wind*?

2. How much can you get done on your own, *without* the empowerment of the Holy Spirit? Take time to reflect on what God's Word says in John 6:63; 15:5; Romans 7:18; and Zechariah 4:6.

3. According to Philippians 4:13, what is the source of power God has given you to draw from — moment by moment, day by day? In practical terms, how can you tap into this unlimited power source? (Consider John 15:4-7; Ephesians 3:20; Luke 10:19.)

PRACTICAL APPLICATION

**But be ye doers of the word, and not hearers only,
deceiving your own selves.
— James 1:22**

1. What would your life be like personally without the wind of the Spirit?

2. When the wind of the Holy Spirit begins to blow, things begin to change! Think back to a time in your life when God showed up like a *rushing mighty wind*. In what ways did the Holy Spirit visibly show up and bring positive change to a negative situation you were in? How does remembering His divine assistance encourage you to trust Him for help in your current circumstances?

3. Do you feel stagnant inside? Has the contamination of this sinful world polluted your soul and spirit? Take time now to pray and ask the Holy Spirit to blow like a rushing, mighty wind in your life — energizing and empowering you to move out of the doldrums of defeat and despair and into the light of His joy and peace.

TOPIC

The Holy Spirit: Gift

SCRIPTURES

1. **Acts 2:38,39** — Then Peter said unto them, Repent, and be baptized every one of you in the name of Jesus Christ for the remission of sins, and ye shall receive the gift of the Holy Ghost. For the promise is unto you, and to your children, and to all that are afar off, even as many as the Lord our God shall call.

GREEK WORDS

1. "repent" — **μετανοέω** (*metanoeo*): pictures a change of mind that results in a complete, radical, total change of behavior; a decision to completely change or to entirely turn around in the way that one is thinking, believing, or living; a total transformation affecting every part of a person's life, both inside and outside, resulting in a behavioral change

2. "remission" — **ἄφεσις** (*aphesis*): a release from the effects of broken-ness; to set free; to release; to permanently dismiss; to send away with no option to ever retrieve again; to loosen from the detrimental effects of sickness or shatteredness

3. "receive" — **λαμβάνω** (*lambano*): to seize or to lay hold of something in order to make it one's very own, almost like a person who reaches out to grab, capture, or take possession of something; depicts one who graciously receives something that is freely and easily given

4. "gift" — **δωρεά** (*dorea*): a gift that is freely given and not acquired by merit or entitlement; a gift given freely; a gift given gratuitously

SYNOPSIS

Several decades ago — in the sixties, seventies, and early eighties — the gifts of the Holy Spirit were manifesting considerably in many denominational churches and arena meetings. Tongues, interpretation of tongues, words of knowledge, healings, and miracles were commonplace. But something happened along the way that has greatly diminished and restricted the movement of the Spirit. God wants to see this change, and it can! Anyone who welcomes the gift of the Holy Spirit and makes room for Him to move will experience His tangible, supernatural presence once again.

The emphasis of this lesson:

The Holy Spirit is a gift that's freely given to every believer the moment they repent of their sin and make Jesus the Lord of their life. This gift cannot be acquired by entitlement or merit. It's freely given and is the most amazing gift you'll ever receive in your life.

A Summary of the First Nine Symbols of the Holy Spirit

Thus far, we have examined nine symbols of the Holy Spirit. Before we look at our tenth symbol, let's quickly review each expression of the Spirit we've learned about in the first five lessons.

1. **OIL.** Symbolically, the Holy Spirit is depicted in Scripture as *oil*. This is the number one metaphor of the Spirit, and it appears more than 200 times.
2. **DEW.** We saw in Psalm 133 that the Holy Spirit is depicted as the morning *dew*, which is an accurate description of how He works. Moisture is in the air at all times but can't always be seen. Yet, when the right atmospheric conditions are met and the dew point is reached, the moisture in the air suddenly manifests as *dew* on every-thing — every blade of grass, every tree, every piece of furniture.

In the same way, the Holy Spirit is present at all times but is often undetected. Yet, when the right spiritual conditions are met, the Spirit will suddenly begin manifesting on everyone that is present. Psalm 133 reveals that *believers dwelling together in unity* as the spiritual condition needed to unleash the corporate anointing of the Holy Spirit.

When we come together in unity, suddenly the Spirit shows up every-where, touching everyone. That's what we see in Acts 2:1. The Bible says, "…They were all with one accord in one place," then the Holy Spirit descended and filled everyone in the room with His power. Unity is the key that unlocks the dew-like corporate anointing of the Spirit.

3. **RAIN**. Under the inspiration of the Spirit of God, the prophet Joel prophesied that there would be an *early rain* and a *latter rain* of the Holy Spirit (*see* Joel 2:23). In Israel, there were early rains that usually came in October and November to loosen the soil and prepare it to receive the seed. There were also latter rains that occurred in March and April that caused the crops to grow and be ready for harvest. Metaphorically, Joel compared these rains with the outpouring of the Holy Spirit: the early rain of the Spirit came at the time of Pentecost, and the latter rain will take place at the very end of the Church age, which is our time.

4. **A RIVER**. The Holy Spirit is also symbolically portrayed in Scripture as *a river*. Jesus Himself referred to the Spirit in this way in John 7:38 when He said, "He that believeth on me, as the scripture hath said, out of his belly shall flow rivers of living water...." That word for "living water" in Greek describes *water that is alive and filled with vibrancy and life*. Not only will living water nourish us, it will also "flow" out of us and feed others. The Greek word for "flow" here is *rheo*, which pictures *a rushing stream, so full that it overflows its banks*.

   The river of the Spirit is so powerful it has the ability to move debris out of the way. We also noted that there are different types of rivers. There are shallow rivers, which are usually noisy, and there are deep rivers, which are quieter and very powerful. Psalm 46:4 (*NIV*) says, "There is a river whose streams make glad the city of God...." Just as a river sometimes flows into different streams, the Holy Spirit is made up of different streams that all make glad the city of God.

5. **WATER**. In Isaiah 44:3 (*NIV*), God said, "For I will pour *water* upon the thirsty land and streams on the dry ground; I will pour out my *Spirit* on your offspring, and my blessing on your descendants." God promises to pour His Spirit out like water upon anyone who is thirsty. For we "...have been all made to drink into one Spirit" (1 Corinthians 12:13).

   The word "drink" here is the Greek word *potidzo*, which literally means *to drink; consume; or imbibe*. It carries the idea of *being completely flooded or irrigated* by God's Spirit. This is His intention for us as we drink the *water* of the Holy Spirit. Even if we've been parched and barren, God promises to thoroughly irrigate our lives so we can once again produce fruit.

6. **FIRE**. In Lesson 4, we learned that the Holy Spirit is also symbolized as *fire*. John the Baptist identified Jesus as the one who would baptize us with the Holy Ghost and with fire (*see* Matthew 3:16). This prophecy began to be fulfilled in Acts 2:1-4, which describes the Holy Spirit descending on the disciples in the Upper Room on the Day of Pentecost. Verse 3 says, "And there appeared unto them cloven tongues like as of *fire*, and it sat upon each of them."

   Just as fire drives engines and moves ships, when the Holy Spirit comes as *fire*, He empowers us with divine energy to do what God has called us to do. As *fire*, the Spirit also purifies us and removes rubbish from our lives so that we can serve Him unhindered. Without the fire of the Holy Spirit, life would be a very cold, dark place spiritually.

7. **A DOVE**. All four gospels tell about the baptism of Jesus in the Jordan River and indicate that the moment He came up out of the water, the heavens were opened and the Holy Spirit descended on Him *"like a dove."* The Bible doesn't say the Holy Spirit *is* a dove; it says He is *like a dove*, which means when He speaks to us and deals with us, He is gentle and tender like a dove.

8. **CLOTHING**. In Luke 24:49, Jesus said to His disciples, "…Tarry ye in the city of Jerusalem, until ye be endued with power from on high." The word "endued" here is the Greek word *enduo*, which means *to be clothed; to array, clothe, endue, or to put on*. This word carries the idea of *sinking into a garment* and depicts *one who is so comfortable in his clothing, he sinks into it*. Hence, the word *"enduo"* is the Greek word for *a new set of clothes*. God wants us to become so comfortable in His power that we sink right into it — like a familiar environment in which we live. The power of the Holy Spirit is to be every believer's new surroundings.

9. **WIND**. In our last lesson, we saw how *wind* has helped shape civilization into what we see today. In addition to driving ships that transported the early explorers to new lands, wind has also been instrumental in keeping the world from being a stagnant place filled with pollution and the stench of decay. Just as we're dependent on the natural wind for our existence, we're also dependent on the supernatural *wind* of the Holy Spirit for power and progress.

   Jesus talked about this during His conversation with Nicodemus in John 3, and it is also mentioned by Luke in Acts 2 when he described the arrival of the Holy Spirit as a "rushing mighty wind." Although we can't see the Holy Spirit, we can feel His effects as He begins to blow like wind and bring change. When the Spirit moves upon a person or a church, suddenly they come alive and begin to make forward progress. Instead of resisting Him and being blown away, we can choose to catch His wind in our sails and allow Him to propel us to the place He wants us to be. If we're going to make any forward progress and have the stench of stagnation removed from our lives, we must have the wind of the Holy Spirit.

True Repentance Is Decision

How else is the Holy Spirit depicted in Scripture? He is also referred to as a *gift*. In Acts 2:38, the Bible says, "Then Peter said unto them, Repent, and be baptized every one of you in the name of Jesus Christ for the remission of sins, and ye shall receive the *gift* of the Holy Ghost."

Notice the first word out of Peter's mouth — "repent." It is the Greek word *metanoeo*, which pictures *a change of mind that results in a complete, radical, total change of behavior*. It is *a decision to completely change or to entirely turn around in the way that one is thinking, believing, or living*. It denotes *a total transformation affecting every part of a person's life, both inside and outside, resulting in a behavioral change*.

What is interesting is that the Greek word for "repent" — *metanoeo* — is very similar to the Greek word *metamelomai*, which is the word used to describe Judas Iscariot's reaction after he betrayed Jesus. The Bible says, "...When he [Judas] saw that he [Jesus] was condemned, *repented* himself, and brought again the thirty pieces of silver to the chief priests and elders" (Matthew 27:3). The word "repented" here is *metamelomai*, which means *to feel sorrow, regret, and guilt*. What Judas experienced was not true repentance.

It is important to note that the word *metanoeo* — translated here as "repent" — comes from two Greek words: the word *meta*, which describes *a change* or *transformation*; and the word *nous*, which is the word for *the mind*. There is no mention of emotions being involved at all. Although we may experience some emotion, it is not required. Repentance is totally *a decision of one's mind and will*. That is why years ago when churches and ministries reported how many salvations had taken place through their efforts, they usually reported them as *decisions* for Christ. Again, repentance is a decision.

Repentance Positions Us
To Receive the Gift of the Holy Spirit

Peter said that anyone who makes the decision to repent will receive the "remission of sins" (Acts 2:38). This word "remissions" is the Greek word *aphesis*, which means *to set free; to release;* or *to permanently dismiss.* It can also be translated *to send away with no option to ever retrieve again; to loosen from the detrimental effects of sickness or shatteredness; to release from the effects of brokenness.*

The use of this word tells us that when you have received the "remission of sins," (forgiveness), you are *permanently set free from past sins.* God dismisses them from you and sends them away, never to retrieve them again. This wonderful promise is confirmed in Psalm 103:12, which says, "As far as the east is from the west, so far hath he removed our transgressions from us." East and west will never meet, which means when God dismisses your sins, they are gone forever. Praise God!

Along with the remission of sins, Peter said, "…and ye shall receive the *gift* of the Holy Ghost" (Acts 2:38). The word "receive" here is the Greek word *lambano,* which means *to seize or to lay hold of something in order to make it one's very own, almost like a person who reaches out to grab, capture, or take possession of something.* This word *lambano* depicts *one who graciously receives something that is freely and easily given.*

What does God want us to graciously seize and lay hold of and make our very own? It is "the gift of the Holy Ghost." In Greek, the word "gift" is *dorea,* and it describes *a gift that is freely given and not acquired by merit or entitlement; a gift given freely;* or *a gift given gratuitously. Dorea* is the exact same word used in Ephesians 2:8, which says, "For by grace are ye saved through faith; and that not of yourselves: it is the *gift* of God."

God's *gift* to you is the Holy Spirit, and it is the most marvelous *gift* you'll ever receive. Every person receives this gift the moment he or she fully surrenders to the Lordship of Jesus and repents of sin. In fact, Peter went on to say, "For the promise is unto you, and to your children, and to all that are afar off, even as many as the Lord our God shall call" (Acts 2:39).

Friend, God wants you to totally unwrap the gift of the Holy Spirit and explore everything about Him. In our next lesson, we will look at another facet of the Holy Spirit's work in our lives — His function as a divine *seal* and an *earnest*.

STUDY QUESTIONS

Study to shew thyself approved unto God, a workman that needeth not to be ashamed, rightly dividing the word of truth.
— 2 Timothy 2:15

1. In your own words, describe the difference between true repentance (the Greek word *metanoeo*) and false repentance (the Greek word *metamelomai*).

2. According to Second Corinthians 7:9 and 10, true repentance results from *godly sorrow*, not worldly sorrow. How do these two types of sorrow differ from each other? What does each one produce in our lives?

PRACTICAL APPLICATION

But be ye doers of the word, and not hearers only,
deceiving your own selves.
— James 1:22

1. The moment you repent of sin, you are *immediately* forgiven (*see* 1 John 1:9). God's Word says, "As far as the east is from the west, so far hath he removed our transgressions from us" (Psalm 103:12). How does knowing that God forever dismisses your sins encourage you and instill gratefulness in your heart?

2. Knowing that repentance is a decision of the mind and will, it is sometimes a *process* that takes time before the full effects are experienced. In what areas of your life can you see that repentance has done a full work? What area(s) are you still working through the process of repentance?

3. The Bible says that the Holy Spirit is a *gift* to every believer. How has the Holy Spirit personally been a gift to you? What new aspects of His character has He recently unwrapped for you?

TOPIC

The Holy Spirit: Seal and Earnest

SCRIPTURES

1. **Ephesians 1:13,14** — In whom ye also trusted, after that ye heard the word of truth, the gospel of your salvation: in whom also after that ye believed, ye were sealed with that Holy Spirit of promise, which is the earnest of our inheritance until the redemption of the purchased possession, unto the praise of his glory.

2. **2 Corinthian 1:22** — Who hath also sealed us, and given the earnest of the Spirit in our hearts.

GREEK WORDS

1. "sealed" — **σφραγίζω** (*sphragidzo*): pictures a seal placed on a package after the product had been thoroughly examined and inspected to make sure it was fully intact and complete; the seal was proof the product was impeccable; normally such seals bore the insignia of a wealthy or famous person, which meant that this package was to be treated with tender care; the seal affirmed who was the owner and guaranteed the package would make it to its final destination

2. "earnest" — **ἀρραβὼν** (*arrabon*): a payment given in advance to guarantee the whole amount will be paid afterward; earnest-money; an installment; a deposit; a down-payment which guarantees full delivery of a promise; security deposit given by the purchaser to assure confidence and peace to the seller that he will fulfill his promise

SYNOPSIS

Jesus said that we are the light of the world — a light that should not be hidden in any way (*see* Matthew 5:14). He said, "Neither do men light a candle, and put it under a bushel, but on a candlestick; and it giveth light unto all that are in the house (Matthew 5:15).

The word "candle" in this verse doesn't refer to a traditional candle you might think of. It was actually a small lamp filled with oil. These lamps were often made of clay and had a hole in their top so they could be refilled with oil. On one side was a small circular handle a person could slip their finger through, and on the other side was a spout-like opening referred to as the mouth. A wick ran down the mouth of the lamp into a reservoir of oil and was set on fire to provide light. As long as there was oil in the lamp, the wick kept burning and brought light to anyone that was in darkness.

Jesus compared each of us to a lamp like this. We are designed by God to carry the oil of the Holy Spirit, and like these lamps, we have a mouth that He desires to ignite with the fire of His Spirit. As we burn brightly and bring light to others, our supply of oil is used and has to be replenished again and again, signifying our need for being continually filled with the Holy Spirit.

Again, Jesus said, "Neither do men light a candle, and put it under a bushel, but on a candlestick..." (Matthew 5:15). Why would a person put a 'lamp' on a 'lampstand'? Because the higher the lamp is, the more effective it is at giving its light. A lamp placed on a table will just illuminate the table. But a lamp placed on a lampstand will shine more light and dispel more darkness. And that's what God wants for us! He wants us to take the oil and fire of the Holy Spirit and allow Him to elevate us to a place where His light can have the maximum impact!

The emphasis of this lesson:

The Bible declares that as a believer, you have been sealed with the Holy Spirit. You have been thoroughly examined by God and found flawless. Therefore, He has deposited His Spirit in you as an earnest or down payment of even greater things that are still to come.

A Summary of Ten Symbols of the Holy Spirit

Can you recall the ten Symbols of the Holy Spirit from the Old and New Testament that we've studied so far? Here is a quick recap to refresh your memory:

The Holy Spirit is metaphorically depicted as...

1. **OIL** – Over 200 times in Scripture, the Holy Spirit is referred to as anointing *oil*.

2. **DEW** – When unity emerges among God's people, the anointing of the Holy Spirit manifests on everyone like the morning *dew* (Psalm 133).

3. **RAIN** – The Holy Spirit is portrayed as the *early and latter rains* that come at just the right time with the exact amount of spiritual rain we need to help us grow (Joel 2:23).

4. **A RIVER** – The Holy Spirit is also likened to *a river* that floods us with new life and washes away anything that's resistant to His will being done on earth as it is in Heaven (John 7:37,38).

5. **WATER** – God promised to give the *water* of the Holy Spirit to anyone who is thirsty. Only He can completely quench our spiritual thirst (Isaiah 44:3).

6. **FIRE** – The Holy Spirit also comes to work in us like an all-consuming *fire*. He purifies our lives, burns up the rubbish, and empowers us to move forward in life (Matthew 3:11; Acts 2:3).

7. **A DOVE** – When Jesus was baptized in the Jordan River, the Holy Spirit descended upon Him like *a dove*. This describes His gentleness and tenderness in the way that He operates in our lives (Matthew 3:16).

8. **CLOTHING** – The Bible says we are to be "endued" with power from on high. In Greek, "endued" describes *a brand new set of clothing* that becomes so comfortable one simply sinks into it. God's intention is for us to sink into the power of the Holy Spirit and learn to be comfortable in Him (Luke 24:49).

9. **WIND** – On the Day of Pentecost, the Holy Spirit descended as a rushing, mighty *wind*. When He operates as *wind*, we can't see Him, but we can feel the effects of His presence. (John 3:8; Acts 2:2).

10. **A GIFT** – God wants us to graciously lay hold of the *gift* of the Holy Ghost and make Him our very own. He is a *gift* that's freely given and can't be acquired by merit or entitlement (Acts 2:38).

We Are 'Sealed' With the Holy Spirit

In what other ways is the Holy Spirit symbolized? The Bible describes Him as a *seal* and the *earnest* of our inheritance. The apostle Paul talked about the Spirit in this way in his letter to the church of Ephesus, saying, "In whom ye also trusted, after that ye heard the word of truth, the gospel of your salvation: in whom also after that ye believed, ye were sealed with that Holy Spirit of promise" (Ephesians 1:13).

In this verse, we see a description of the miracle of salvation. The moment we heard the word of truth — the gospel message — and we put out faith in Christ, something extraordinary happened. Paul said we "…were sealed with the Holy Spirit of promise." The word "sealed" is the Greek word *sphragidzo*, which describes *a seal placed on a package after the product had been thoroughly examined and inspected to make sure it was fully intact and complete.* The seal was proof that the product was impeccable.

In Greek and Roman times — and in some places still today — if a package was going to be dispatched to another location, it first went through a series of investigations to make sure the contents were not flawed, broken, or shattered. This examination process could be very laborious, but if everything was intact, the sender would close up the package, pour hot wax onto its crease, and then carefully press the owner's insignia ring into the wax.

This seal affirmed who the owner was, and normally such seals bore the insignia of a wealthy or famous person, which meant that the package was to be treated with utmost care. Once that waxed insignia was placed on a package, it was "sealed" and signified that all the contents were in perfect order. No one would dare break into a package sealed with the insignia of a powerful owner — especially if the owner was a high-ranking official. The seal was like the most expensive, secure postage stamp you could put on a package. The consequences of breaking into such a package and disturbing its contents were very severe. Thus, the seal guaranteed that the package would be delivered to its ultimate destination.

All this meaning is packed into the word *sphragidzo* — translated as "sealed" in Ephesians 1:13. Under the inspiration of the Holy Spirit, Paul used this word to describe what takes place the moment we put our faith in Jesus Christ and are born again. Jesus places His insignia on us in the seal of the Holy Spirit. He is the owner to whom we belong.

This also tells us that when we were born again, God thoroughly examined everything inside our heart to make sure we were made completely new. Through the miraculous work of the Holy Spirit, we were made a new creation in Christ (*see* 2 Corinthians 5:17); God found no flaws, no defects, and no shattered places in us. Once He confirmed our perfect condition in Christ, we were sealed with the gift of His Spirit and branded as His own.

Figuratively speaking, Jesus poured His spiritual wax on you and pressed the insignia of the Holy Spirit into you. Through the Spirit's indwelling presence, you have guaranteed proof that you belong to God *and* that you will make it all the way to your ultimate destination, which is Heaven. That's what the word "sealed" means. Even if you've had some bumps and detours along the way, the seal of the Holy Spirit on your life is God's guarantee that you will make it all the way to your heavenly home.

Taking into account the original Greek meaning, here is the *Renner Interpretive Version (RIV)* of Ephesians 1:13:

> **When you were placed in Christ, God stamped you with a special seal and embossed it so deeply that it cannot be broken, erased, rubbed out, wiped out, deleted, or removed; THAT unbreakable seal is the Holy Spirit. Once you were stamped with Him, it meant you had God's approval. He examined the contents of your heart and found nothing flawed or inferior.**

> **And because everything was in order, He stamped you with the Holy Spirit, which is His seal of approval. Anyone who has this stamp is headed for special treatment. THIS seal means you belong to God and no one is to interfere with you as a "package."**

> **This 'Holy Spirit stamp' means the postage is prepaid to get you all the way to your ultimate destination. That means you can be sure that once your journey with the Lord begins, you are going to make it all the way to where God wants you to go! As good as all of this already seems, it's only the beginning of what God has planned for us.**

The Holy Spirit Is Also Our 'Earnest'

In Ephesians 1:14, Paul went on to say that the Holy Spirit, "…is the *earnest* of our inheritance until the redemption of the purchased possession, unto the praise of his glory." So in addition to being our *seal*, the Holy Spirit is also the "*earnest* of our inheritance."

The word "earnest" is the Greek word *arrabon*, which describes *a payment given in advance to guarantee the whole amount will be paid afterward.* It denotes *earnest-money; an installment; a deposit; a down-payment, which guarantees full delivery of a promise.* Furthermore, the word *arrabon* depicts *a security deposit given by the purchaser to assure confidence and peace to the seller that he will fulfill his promise.*

Taking into account the original Greek meaning, here is the *Renner Interpretive Version (RIV)* of Ephesians 1:14:

> **As good as all of this already seems, it's only the beginning of all that God has planned for us! The Holy Spirit is just the first-installment of the incredible things that God has planned as a part of our full inheritance. You might say the Holy Spirit is God's "down-payment" to show that He is serious and intends to complete the deal, finalize all the papers, put the product in His name, and finally make us His very own possession, with no one else having the ability to exercise any claims or liens against us. When this process is finally wrapped up and the deal is completely sealed, we're going to all want to stand up and give God a round of applause for everything accomplished in our lives through His glory!**

What's interesting is that Paul also used the words "sealed" and "earnest" to describe the gift of the Holy Spirit in Second Corinthians 1:22. He said, "[God] who hath also sealed us, and given the earnest of the Spirit in our hearts."

Taking into account the original Greek meanings, here is the *Renner Interpretive Version (RIV)* of Second Corinthians 1:22:

> **Who has stamped us with a special seal and embossed it so deeply that it cannot be broken, erased, rubbed out, wiped out, deleted or removed. Because we have that seal, it means we have God's approval. He has examined the contents of our hearts, found nothing flawed or inferior, and stamped us with the Holy Spirit as His seal of approval. Because we have this stamp, the postage has been prepaid to get us all the way to our ultimate destination. So we can be sure that once our journey with the Lord begins, we are going to make it all the way to where God wants us to go!**

Friend, if you've said "yes" to Jesus and made Him the Lord of your life, God sees you as flawless! He has thoroughly examined your heart and placed His *seal* of approval on you in the form of the Holy Spirit. The Spirit's presence in your life is the *earnest* or *down payment* that guarantees you have been bought by God and you are going to make it all the way into eternity with Him!

In our next lesson, we will examine two more symbols of the Holy Spirit that are particularly used in the New Testament. They are "glory" and "light."

STUDY QUESTIONS

Study to shew thyself approved unto God, a workman that needeth not to be ashamed, rightly dividing the word of truth.
— 2 Timothy 2:15

1. The Bible says you are "sealed" with the Holy Spirit, and the Spirit's indwelling presence is proof that you belong to God *and* that you will make it all the way to your ultimate destination, which is Heaven. What does the Bible say in Jude 1:24 and Second Timothy 1:12 that confirms this? (Also consider 1 Thessalonians 3:3 and Jesus' prayer in John 17:9,11,12,15.)

2. The Holy Spirit is also an "earnest" or *down payment* in your life, showing that God is serious and intends to complete the deal He initiated. What has God specifically promised to do for you in Philippians 1:6 and First Thessalonians 5:23 and 24? How do these passages confirm that the Holy Spirit is working as an "earnest" in your life?

PRACTICAL APPLICATION

But be ye doers of the word, and not hearers only, deceiving your own selves.
— James 1:22

1. The gift of salvation is truly a miracle! Can you remember the moment you surrendered your life to Jesus and made Him your Savior and Lord? What events did God allow to take place in your life to soften your heart and lead you to Him? How did He make the truth of the Gospel come alive in your heart and mind?

2. If you had the opportunity to share with a close friend what it means to be "sealed" with the Holy Spirit, what would you say? How might you describe the ancient process of *sealing a package* and relate it to being "sealed" with the Holy Spirit?

3. What is most encouraging to you about the process and purpose of being "sealed" with the Holy Spirit? How does this understanding humble you and move you to worship God for His extravagant kindness and love?

TOPIC

The Holy Spirit: Glory and Light

SCRIPTURES

1. **1 Peter 4:14** — If ye be reproached for the name of Christ, happy are ye; for the spirit of glory and of God resteth upon you: on their part he is evil spoken of, but on your part he is glorified.

2. **2 Corinthians 3:7-11** — But if the ministration of death, written and engraven in stones, was glorious, so that the children of Israel could not stedfastly behold the face of Moses for the glory of his countenance; which glory was to be done away: How shall not the ministration of the spirit be rather glorious? For if the ministration of condemnation be glory, much more doth the ministration of righteousness exceed in glory. For even that which was made glorious had no glory in this respect, by reason of the glory that excelleth. For if that which is done away was glorious, much more that which remaineth is glorious.

3. **2 Corinthians 3:17,18** — Now the Lord is that Spirit: and where the Spirit of the Lord is, there is liberty. But we all, with open face beholding as in a glass the glory of the Lord, are changed into the same image from glory to glory, even as by the Spirit of the Lord.

4. **2 Corinthians 4:3-6** — But if our gospel be hid, it is hid to them that are lost: in whom the god of this world hath blinded the minds of them which believe not, lest the light of the glorious gospel of Christ, who is the image of God, should shine unto them. For we preach not ourselves, but Christ Jesus the Lord; and ourselves your servants for Jesus' sake. For God, who commanded the light to shine out of darkness, hath shined in our hearts, to give the light of the knowledge of the glory of God in the face of Jesus Christ.

5. **Ephesians 1:17** — That the God of our Lord Jesus Christ, the Father of glory, may give unto you the spirit of wisdom and revelation in the knowledge of him.

6. **Ephesians 5:14** — Wherefore he saith, Awake thou that sleepest, and arise from the dead, and Christ shall give thee light.

7. **John 16:13,15** — Howbeit when he... is come, he will guide you into all the truth... He shall take of mine, and shall shew it unto you.

GREEK WORDS

1. "glory" — **δόξα** (*doxa*): pictures brightness; glory; honor; something exalted, majestic; magnificent, resplendent, of great worth; the heavy weight of God's presence; the manifestation of God's presence

2. "was glorious" — **γενήθη ἐν δόξῃ** (*egenethe en doxe*): was produced by glory; came into existence by glory; shows that creativity is released in glory

3. "rather" **μᾶλλον** (*mallon*): much more; comparatively much more; vastly more

4. "much more... exceed" — **πολλῷ μᾶλλον περισσεύει** (*pollu mallon perisseuei*): much more abound, overflow, and flood

5. "the glory that excelleth" — **τῆς ὑπερβαλλούσης δόξης** (*tes huperballouses doxes*): the word **ὑπερβάλλω** (*huperballo*): is something that is above and beyond what is normal; exceeding or surpassing; pictures an archer who aims his arrow at the bullseye, but shoots way over the top; depicts something beyond the range of anything considered normal; something unparalleled

6. "much more" — **πολλῷ μᾶλλον** (*pollo mallon*): much, much more; vastly more; incomparably more

7. "liberty" — **ἐλευθερία** (*eleutheria*): liberty, freedom; a state of freedom from slavery; emancipation

8. "open face" — **ἀνακεκαλυμμένῳ προσώπῳ** (*anakekalummeno prosopo*): perpetually unveiled faces; hence, no hiding or pretending or dishonesty, the Greek tense doesn't refer to a one-time unveiling, but to a veil that, once lifted, remains lifted forever

9. "beholding as in a glass" — **κατοπτρίζομαι** (*katoptridzomai*): to look into a mirror to see an image; to peer intently into a mirror

10. "from glory to glory" — **ἀπὸ δόξης εἰς δόξαν** (*apo doxes eis doxan*): the words **ἀπὸ** (*apo*) and **εἰς** (*eis*); **ἀπὸ** (*apo*): means to depart or to leave,

while εἰς (*eis*): means to enter into; to depart from one realm of glory and to move upward into a new and higher level of glory; taking leave of one realm of glory to move upward into a higher realm of glory

11. "shined" — λάμπω (*lampo*): to shine; pictures a beam of light; a direct beam
12. "light" – φωτισμός (*photismos*): illumination; definite and lasting impression

SYNOPSIS

Throughout the Old and New Testament, we see the Holy Spirit manifesting in the form of the *glory of God*. In Moses' day, the *glory* settled over Mount Sinai in the form of a cloud (*see* Exodus 24:15-17), and it covered the Tent of Meeting and filled the tabernacle (*see* Exodus 40:34). At the beginning of Solomon's reign, the *glory* of God filled the newly built temple (*see* 2 Chronicles 7:1,2), and in Jesus' day, it manifested on the Mount of Transfiguration (*see* Matthew 17:1-6). Indeed, the *glory* of God is a recurring symbol of His Holy Spirit.

Light is also a repeated metaphor throughout Scripture. Again and again, David declared God to be the *light* of his life (*see* Psalm 27:1; 36:9), and Micah said He is our *light* in darkness (*see* Micah 7:8). Jesus Himself said, "…I am the *light* of the world…" (John 8:12), and the apostle John called Him "the *light* of men" (*see* John 1:4). What is the meaning of this imagery of "light" and "glory," and why does God use it to reveal the character of His Spirit?

The emphasis of this lesson:

When the Holy Spirit manifests God's glory, the heavy weight of His presence is felt, discerning and meeting the needs of those present. The Spirit also comes to us in the form of light, bringing illumination that makes a permanent, lasting change in our lives.

12 Symbols of the Holy Spirit We've Explored

In *Lesson 2*, we examined the symbol of *oil* — the most recurring emblem of the Holy Spirit found in Scripture. Every believer receives the anointing *oil* of the Spirit the moment he or she is saved. The Holy Spirit also functions as *dew* in our lives. This is beautifully illustrated in Psalm 133.

In *Lesson 3*, we learned about the early and latter rains in Joel 2:23, which prepare and replenish the soil and mature the seed. *Rain* is the third symbol of the Holy Spirit. Jesus Himself gave us the fourth symbol of the Spirit in John 7:38, likening Him to a *river* of living water that brings life and removes hindrances. This brings us to the fifth emblem of the Spirit, which is *water*. God promised to pour out His Spirit like *water* on the thirsty souls of men who long to have their thirst quenched (*see* Isaiah 44:3).

In *Lesson 4*, we saw that the Holy Spirit is also represented by *fire*, *a dove*, and *clothing*. As a *fire*, He purifies our lives from the rubbish of the flesh and this world and empowers us with divine energy. As *a dove*, the Holy Spirit operates in our lives with gentleness and tenderness. As *clothing*, the Spirit "endues" us with power from on high (*see* Luke 24:49). The word "endued" describes *a set of clothing* that becomes so comfortable we sink right into it. That is how relaxed and at peace Jesus wants us to be with the power of His Spirit.

In *Lesson 5*, we discovered that the Holy Spirit is also like *wind*. Although we can't see wind with our eyes, we can feel its effects all around us. When the *wind* of the Holy Spirit begins to blow, He brings powerful, positive change into our lives. He is truly a *gift* God wants us to fully unwrap and understand, which is what we uncovered in *Lesson 6*.

In *Lesson 7*, we saw in Ephesians 1:13 that the Holy Spirit is a *seal*. The word for "sealed" in verse 13 is the Greek word *sphragidzo*, which describes *a seal placed on a package after the product had been thoroughly examined and inspected to make sure it was fully intact and complete.* The seal was proof that the product was impeccable. It also identified who the owner of the package was and guaranteed its safe arrival at its ultimate destination. This tells us that the moment we are saved, God thoroughly inspects our hearts and finds us perfect and complete. He then seals us (figuratively) with the Holy Spirit, guaranteeing our safe entrance in Heaven. Yes, we may have difficulties in this life, but the seal of the Holy Spirit certifies that we're going to arrive in the presence of God intact.

We also learned from Ephesians 1:14 and Second Corinthians 1:22 that the Holy Spirit is an "earnest." In Greek, the word "earnest" is the word *arrabon*, which describes *a payment given in advance to guarantee the whole amount will be paid afterward.* It denotes *earnest-money; an installment; a deposit; a down-payment, which guarantees full delivery of a promise.* The fact the Holy Spirit is our "earnest" is God's promise to completely finish His work in our lives.

The 'Glory' of God Is the Heaviness of His Presence

Another symbol assigned to the Holy Spirit is *glory*. Through the apostle Peter, God said, "If ye be reproached for the name of Christ, happy are ye; for the spirit of *glory* and of God resteth upon you: on their part he is evil spoken of, but on your part he is glorified" (1 Peter 4:14).

The word "glory" here is the Greek word *doxa*, which pictures *brightness; glory; honor;* or *something exalted*. It can also be translated as *majestic; magnificent, resplendent, or of great worth*. Additionally, the word *doxa* is used in the Old Testament Septuagint to describe *the heavy weight of God's presence*. The *glory of God* was considered to be the manifestation of God's presence. This was sometimes referred to as the Shekinah glory that could be tangibly felt, seen, and experienced.

In Solomon's day, when they dedicated the temple, the Shekinah glory (*doxa*) of God came into the temple, and the presence of His glory was so heavy that the Bible says the priests couldn't enter it to fulfill their priestly duties (*see* 2 Chronicles 7:1,2). This helps us understand how people today will often collapse or fall to the ground when the glory of God touches them during a time of prayer. Although some have fallen over on their own accord for appearance sake, this is a genuine manifestation of God's glory that countless people have experienced.

When we come to the New Testament, the meaning of the "glory" (*doxa*) of God expands. In addition to describing *the heavy, weighty presence of God that is filled with all His goodness*, "glory" also carries the idea of *discernment* or *judgment*. At first glance, this may seem strange, but it is actually very significant. It means that when the glory of God manifests today, the Holy Spirit hovers over all who are gathered, *discerning* and *judging* every need that each individual has. Once the Spirit discerns the needs, He begins to miraculously meet them, distributing to each person out of His rich treasury what they lack.

If someone needs conviction of sin, the Holy Spirit gives them conviction. If someone needs physical healing, He imparts it. If someone needs relational restoration, He releases it. If a person is overwhelmed by brokenness, the Holy Spirit begins to piece together the fractured places of their life. If someone needs a financial breakthrough, He begins to put the people in place to provide the provision. Whatever the need is, the "glory" discerns it and begins to meet it. That is what happens when the Holy Spirit is present as the Spirit of glory.

The Holy Spirit's 'Glory' Is a Flooding, Glorious Presence That Outshines the Law

The apostle Paul wrote about the glory of God in Second Corinthians 3, comparing it to the Old Testament law. He said, "But if the ministration of death, written and engraven in stones, was glorious, so that the children of Israel could not stedfastly behold the face of Moses for the glory of his countenance; which glory was to be done away: how shall not the ministration of the spirit be rather glorious?" (2 Corinthians 3:7,8).

Notice the phrase "was glorious" in verse 7. In Greek it is *egenethe en doxe*, and it means *was produced by glory; came into existence by glory*. The Bible tells us that the Ten Commandments were written on stone tablets by the finger of God, which was quite a glorious demonstration. Thus, the commandments came into existence by God's glory.

Immediately, Paul contrasted the glory of the Ten Commandments with the glory of the new covenant administered by the Holy Spirit, saying, "How shall not the ministration of the spirit be rather glorious?" (2 Corinthians 3:8). The word "rather" in Greek is *mallon*, which *means much more; comparatively much more; vastly more*. Hence, the ministry of the Holy Spirit is *vastly more glorious* than that of the Law.

He went on to say, "For if the ministration of condemnation be glory, much more doth the ministration of righteousness exceed in glory" (2 Corinthians 3:9). The words "much more... exceed" is a translation of the Greek phrase *pollu mallon perisseuei*, which means *much more abound, overflow, and flood*. Interestingly, the word "exceed" is actually derived from a Greek word that was often used to describe *a river so full it was beginning to exceed its banks and flood everything*. The use of this word indicates that the presence of the Holy Spirit is *a flooding, glorious presence*.

To this, Paul added, "For even that which was made glorious had no glory in this respect, by reason of the glory that excelleth" (2 Corinthians 3:10). The word "excelleth" is taken from the Greek word *huperballo* — a compound of the word *huper*, meaning *above and beyond*; and the word *ballo*, meaning *to throw*. When these two words are compounded to form the word *huperballo*, it describes *something that is above and beyond what is normal; something that is exceeding or surpassing.* This word pictures an archer who aims his arrow at the bullseye, but shoots way over the top. Moreover, it depicts *something beyond the range of anything considered normal; something unparalleled.*

In the next verse, Paul continued by saying, "For if that which is done away was glorious, much more that which remaineth is glorious" (2 Corinthians 3:11). In other words, once Christ came and established the new and better covenant through His sacrifice on the Cross, the Old Testament Law was done away with. What He gave us in its place is "much more glorious," which in Greek means *much, much more; vastly more; incomparably more glorious.* Hence, what we have today through the Holy Spirit is incomparably more glorious than what we had through the Law.

Several verses later, Paul made this powerful statement: "Now the Lord is that Spirit: and where the Spirit of the Lord is, there is liberty" (2 Corinthians 3:17). The word "liberty" is the Greek word *eleutheria*, which describes *liberty or freedom.* This is the exact word used to describe *a slave that has been emancipated.* What Paul is saying is that when the Spirit of God begins to work and manifest His glory, people are emancipated — they are set free from bondages in many areas of their lives.

Again, this is what happens when the Holy Spirit comes in the form of "glory." There is a heavy presence of God that can be felt, and it is loaded with every good thing that is needed. As the glorious presence of the Holy Spirit fills the room, He begins to discern the needs in every person, and then He begins to meet those needs, touching and transforming the lives of those who are present.

'Light' Is a Powerful Symbol of God's Spirit

Another major symbol of the Holy Spirit described all through Scripture is *light.* The apostle John declared this again and again, stating, "…God is light, and in him is no darkness at all" (1 John 1:5). The apostle Paul also elaborated on this facet of God's Spirit. In his second letter to the believers at Corinth — and to believers throughout all generations — Paul wrote:

> **"But if our gospel be hid, it is hid to them that are lost: in whom the god of this world hath blinded the minds of them which**

believe not, lest the light of the glorious gospel of Christ, who is the image of God, should shine unto them."

2 Corinthians 4:3,4

The word "blinded" in this verse is very important. It is the Greek word *tuphloo*, which doesn't just depict a person who is unable to see; rather, it vividly portrays *someone who has intentionally had their eyes gouged out and no longer has eyes to see.* This is a clear picture of an unbeliever who cannot see the Gospel until the Holy Spirit supernaturally gives them spiritual eyes to see. How does the Spirit do this? The Bible says He brings them "light." Paul continued:

"For we preach not ourselves, but Christ Jesus the Lord; and ourselves your servants for Jesus' sake. For God, who commanded the light to shine out of darkness, hath shined in our hearts, to give the light of the knowledge of the glory of God in the face of Jesus Christ."

2 Corinthians 4:5,6

Two words appear repeatedly in these four verses. First is the word "shine" or "shined." It is the Greek word *lampo*, which means *to shine*, and it pictures *a direct beam of light.* This tells us that when the Holy Spirit begins to "shine" His light in our lives, it is as if He focuses *a direct beam of light* on the problem that needs to be addressed.

The word "light" also appears multiple times, and it is the Greek word *photismos*, which is from where we get the word *photo*. It describes *a light that is so intensely bright that it makes a permanent, lasting impression.* This means that when the Holy Spirit shines His searchlight on our lives and on the truth of God's Word, He creates such a lasting impression that we're never the same again. Only the Holy Spirit can give us spiritual eyes to see and understand Scripture and know what needs to change in our lives.

The symbols of *light* and *glory* are powerful and important, and in our next lesson, we will turn our attention to how the Holy Spirit manifests as wine.

STUDY QUESTIONS

Study to shew thyself approved unto God, a workman that needeth not to be ashamed, rightly dividing the word of truth.
— 2 Timothy 2:15

1. When you think of the "glory of God," what stories or passages in Scripture specifically come to mind? Why do you think these examples stand out to you?

2. The Bible says that Christ established a new, better covenant through His sacrifice on the Cross, and it is incomparably more glorious than the Old Testament Law, which has been done away with. In your own words, describe how our new covenant with God through Jesus is far superior to the Old Testament Law of Moses. (Consider Hebrews 9:13-15; 24-28; 10:19-23.)

PRACTICAL APPLICATION

**But be ye doers of the word, and not hearers only,
deceiving your own selves.
—James 1:22**

1. Have you ever been in a worship service when the "glory" (*doxa*) of the Holy Spirit manifested? In what specific ways was the heavy presence of God's glory felt, seen, or experienced by the people? What needs did He meet? How did the Holy Spirit personally touch *you*?

2. Second Corinthians 3:17 says, "…Where the Spirit of the Lord is, there is liberty." In what areas of your life have you already experienced the marvelous emancipation power of the Holy Spirit? In what areas are you still bound and need the Holy Spirit to bring freedom? Pause and pray: *"Holy Spirit, what practical steps can I take to cooperate with You and experience freedom in my life?"*

3. Name at least two areas of your life where the Holy Spirit has shined an intensely bright light of truth. How have His actions made *a permanent, lasting impression* on you? What has forever changed in your thinking and/or behavior?

TOPIC

The Holy Spirit: Wine

SCRIPTURES

1. **Acts 2:15** — For these are not drunken, as ye suppose....

2. **Ephesians 5:17-21** — Wherefore be ye not unwise, but understanding what the will of the Lord is. And be not drunk with wine, wherein is excess; but be filled with the Spirit; speaking to yourselves in psalms and hymns and spiritual songs, singing and making melody in your heart to the Lord; giving thanks always for all things unto God and the Father in the name of our Lord Jesus Christ; submitting yourselves one to another in the fear of God.

3. **Luke 5:37,38** — And no man putteth new wine into old bottles; else the new wine will burst the bottles, and be spilled, and the bottles shall perish. But new wine must be put into new bottles; and both are preserved.

4. **Psalm 51:7,10** — Purge me with hyssop, and I shall be clean: wash me, and I shall be whiter than snow... Create in me a clean heart, O God; and renew a right spirit within me.

GREEK WORDS

There are no Greek words in this lesson.

SYNOPSIS

Altogether, we have examined 14 symbols used to depict the Holy Spirit in the Old and the New Testament. First, we saw that the Spirit is portrayed as anointing *oil* more than 200 times. In Psalm 133, we saw the Spirit of God compared with *dew*. Then in Joel 2:23, the Holy Spirit is likened unto *rain* that comes in the right amount at the right time. The fourth symbol of the Spirit is *a river* of living water, and it was described by Jesus in John 7:38.

In Isaiah 44:3, the Holy Spirit is depicted as *water*, which God gives to those who are spiritually thirsty. The sixth emblem of the Spirit is *a dove*, which is how He manifested at Jesus' baptism (*see* Matthew 3:16). *Fire* is yet another symbol, and it was demonstrated on the Day of Pentecost when the disciples were baptized in the Holy Spirit and *fire* (*see* Acts 2:3).

When we come to Luke 24:49, we see the Holy Spirit's power likened unto spiritual *clothing* that encapsulates and energizes us. Then in John 3:8 and Acts 2:2, we saw the Spirit described as *wind* that freely moves where it wills. The tenth symbol of the Holy Spirit is mentioned by the apostle Peter in Acts 2:38, who said the Spirit is a *gift* to us that God wants us to unwrap and fully explore.

In Ephesians 1:13 and 14, we discovered that the Holy Spirit is also our *seal* and our *earnest*. The moment we were saved, God thoroughly examined and approved us and gave us the Holy Spirit as a down payment of the things to come. Then in our last program, we saw the Holy Spirit metaphorically portrayed as *glory* and *light*.

The emphasis of this lesson:

Metaphorically, the Holy Spirit is also described as *wine*, which produces intoxicating effects when we drink of Him. God wants us to become 'professional drinkers' that are continually filled with the 'wine' of His Spirit.

The Wine of the Spirit
Was First Poured Out on the Day of Pentecost

The last symbol of the Holy Spirit we are going to look at is the emblem of *wine*. In several places, the Bible indirectly likens the Spirit to *wine*, and the first place we see this is on the Day of Pentecost. When the Holy Spirit descended on the disciples like a rushing mighty wind and cloven tongues of fire, the disciples who were gathered in the Upper Room "…were all filled with the Holy Ghost, and began to speak with other tongues, as the Spirit gave them utterance" (Acts 2:4).

When the multitude of travelers who were in Jerusalem for the feast heard the uproar of the disciples, they were dumfounded. "Others mocking said, These men are full of new wine" (Acts 2:13). In other words, they said, "These guys are drunk," which was certainly not the case. Moved by the Holy Spirit, Peter stood up and declared, "For these are *not* drunken, as ye suppose…" (Acts 2:15). He then proceeded to tell them that what they were hearing was what was prophesied by the prophet Joel — God was pouring out His Spirit!

What's amazing is that the devout Jewish men from every nation heard the disciples speaking about the wonderful works of God in their own native dialects. But how could this be? How could thousands of people from over a dozen different regions clearly hear praise to God in their own native tongue?

The answer is simple. The miracle didn't happen in the mouths of the speakers; the miracle happened in the ears of the hearers. Again and again in Acts 2, the listeners made statements like, "…How hear we every man in our own tongue, wherein we were born?" (Acts 2:8). By the time the language of tongues reached the ears of the listeners, the Holy Spirit had supernaturally translated the words so that each person could hear the wonders of God in their own language!

Indeed, when we begin to drink of the wine of the Holy Spirit, we come under His influence, and it affects our behavior in amazing ways.

It's God's Will That You 'Be Filled With the Spirit'

The apostle Paul elaborated on the Holy Spirit being a symbol of wine in his letter to the Ephesian believers. Speaking to them candidly about their example of Christian living, Paul told them, "Wherefore be ye not unwise, but understanding what the will of the Lord is" (Ephesians 5:17). Stop for a moment and reread Paul's instructions. He said, "Understand what the will of the Lord is." Then in the next several verses, he clearly unpacked God's will for their lives — and for ours.

The first thing Paul said was, "And be not drunk with wine, wherein is excess; but be filled with the Spirit" (Ephesians 5:18). In Greek, the phrase "be not drunk with wine" is a very strong prohibition. It is the equivalent of Paul saying, "Stop getting drunk with wine, and stop it now!" Paul's strong warning here indicates the Ephesian believers were drinking way too much. In fact, they were drinking to the point of intoxication.

This brings up an important question: why do people usually drink? The answer is they like the way it makes them feel. It helps them temporarily forget about the pain of life, and for many, being intoxicated lifts their spirit. It's amazing how alcohol alters a person's personality. When someone is drunk, they will say and do things they would not normally say or do. Their inhibitions are removed, making them bolder and unrestrained in their actions, causing them to do things they later regret.

Although the effects of drinking can be temporarily gratifying, Paul urged the Ephesian believers to stop getting drunk with wine and stop it immediately. With his strong warning, he offered them a healthy alternative: "…But be filled with the Spirit" (Ephesians 5:18). When we are filled with the Holy Spirit, something incredible happens. Just like imbibing excessive amounts of alcohol changes us, drinking of the Spirit changes us too — but in a positive way. It enlivens our faith, makes us bolder, and enables us to do and say things we wouldn't normally do and say. Indeed, being filled with the Holy Spirit has an intoxicating effect that is truly transforming.

The Wine of the Spirit Produces Intoxicating Effects

As Paul continued his letter to the Ephesians, he began to describe the effects of being filled with the Spirit. He said that when you are filled with the Spirit, you begin "speaking to yourselves in psalms and hymns and spiritual songs, singing and making melody in your heart to the Lord" (Ephesians 5:19). So being filled with the Holy Spirit releases such joy and peace in us that we have a perpetual song inside our hearts.

But that's not all. When we're filled with the Holy Spirit, Paul said we begin "giving thanks always for all things unto God and the Father in the name of our Lord Jesus Christ" (Ephesians 5:20). Imagine that! Instead of griping and complaining about everything, the wine of the Spirit transforms our perspective and makes us thankful for God's goodness.

But there's more. Paul went on to say that when you are filled with the Holy Spirit, you begin "submitting yourselves one to another in the fear of God" (Ephesians 5:21). In other words, one of the intoxicating effects of the wine of the Spirit is liberation from pride and a willingness to submit to fellow believers. Wow! With positive effects like these, it is no wonder Paul urged us to be filled with the Holy Spirit.

Become a Professional Drinker

Looking again at Paul's instructions in Ephesians 5:18, he said, "And be not drunk with wine, wherein is excess; but be filled with the Spirit." In Greek, the verb tense of the phrase "be filled" is extremely important. It would more accurately be translated, "Be being filled." In other words, we are to be *continually* filled with the Holy Spirit.

God wants us to become *professional drinkers*! He wants us to develop the habit of feasting on His Word and drinking of His Spirit every day. Remember, Paul said we "...have been all made to drink into one Spirit" (1 Corinthians 12:13). So we have a God-given ability to drink of the wine of the Holy Spirit and experience the life-giving effects He brings.

Just as people who regularly drink wine become controlled by it, the more we drink of the Spirit, the more we become controlled by Him. That is why Paul went on to say, "Pray at all times (on every occasion, in every season) **in the Spirit**, with all [manner of] prayer and entreaty... (Ephesians 6:18 *AMPC*). Praying in the Spirit is drinking of the Spirit! And the intoxicating effects it produces are amazing!

What Kind of Container Are You?

When it comes to storing wine, there are basically two types of containers. There are *vases* and *wineskins* — and it's important for us to know the difference between these two and know which one God wants us to be.

Vases were used for fermenting and long-term storage. They were very large and quite heavy. In fact, vases were so heavy it usually took at least two men to carry one, which is why they were only used for fermenting and storing wine. Vases were not something you would walk around with and drink from or use to serve wine to others. Their sheer size and weight made it impossible.

The truth is, many individuals are functioning like vases. They have been baptized in the Holy Spirit and have received His marvelous infilling, but all they do is collect and store the Spirit's wine. The same is true of many churches. They have experienced many powerful moves of God's Spirit over the years and have allowed the wine of the Spirit to collect and ferment, becoming stronger and stronger. But because all they do is receive and never share with others, they have no capacity to receive anything new. God never intended for us to be vases. He wants us to be wineskins.

Wineskins were small and made out of leather. They were meant to be filled and carry small amounts of wine that could be shared with others. And because wineskins didn't hold much, they had to be refilled over and over again.

Jesus used the wineskin as an illustration of what we are supposed to be. We are to carry the wine of the Spirit and share it with others everywhere we go. Then we are to be refilled again and again with a fresh supply of the Holy Spirit, continually sharing what we have with others. A vase cannot be refilled because it's made to store wine. Again, God doesn't want us to be vases that just hold what we receive; He wants us to be wineskins that are constantly replenished with a new filling.

Old Wineskins Can Be Made New Again

It's important to note that over time, wineskins could become hard and no longer usable if not properly maintained. This is what Jesus was referring to in Luke 5:37 and 38 when He said, "And no man putteth new wine into old bottles; else the new wine will burst the bottles, and be spilled, and the bottles shall perish. But new wine must be put into new bottles; and both are preserved."

During New Testament times, the juice from freshly pressed grapes was placed in new wineskins. Yeast naturally occurring in the skins began to break down the sugar in the juice into alcohol and carbon dioxide — a process known as fermentation. This made the new wineskins expand. Over time, as the bags aged, they would become stretched out, rigid, and even crack. Thus, old wineskins were no longer able to receive new wine due to the stretching that was required of the wineskins. If new wine was placed in old wineskins, they would burst during fermentation, spilling the valuable new wine and destroying the wineskins. That is why Jesus said, "No one puts new wine into old wineskins."

The good news is that if a wineskin became old and rigid, it could be renewed and made usable again. To do this, the old wineskin had to be scrubbed thoroughly again and again. Next, it had to be beaten in order to make it soft again. Then it had to be washed thoroughly. After that, the wineskin was heated in order to shrink it back to its original size and form. If an old wineskin was submitted to this laborious process of scrubbing, beating, washing, and heating, it could be made new again and refilled with new wine.

Spiritually speaking, we are like wineskins that hold the wine of the Holy Spirit, which represents His presence, His moving, and His revelation of truth. Over time we can become stretched out from our service to God and even hardened in our ways. In order to remain pliable and usable in His hands we must be willing to submit ourselves to the process of spiritual *scrubbing, beating, washing, and heating.* If we are willing to submit ourselves to God's dealings with us, we can be made new again and refilled with the wine of His Spirit.

How about you? Have you become like an old wineskin? Do you want to be made new again? If you are willing to submit to God's dealings, pray as David prayed:

> **"Purge me with hyssop, and I shall be clean: wash me, and I shall be whiter than snow.... Create in me a clean heart, O God; and renew a right spirit within me. Cast me not away from thy presence; and take not thy Holy Spirit from me. Restore unto me the joy of thy salvation; and uphold me with thy free spirit."**
> **Psalm 51:7,10-12**

STUDY QUESTIONS

> **Study to shew thyself approved unto God, a workman that needeth not to be ashamed, rightly dividing the word of truth.**
> **— 2 Timothy 2:15**

1. Carefully reflect on Paul's words to the Ephesian believers — *and us* — in Ephesians 5:17-21, and identify what you can expect to happen in your life when you choose to drink of and be filled with the Holy Spirit. Looking at these same verses, what behavior can you also avoid by being filled with the Spirit?

2. God wants you to "pray at all times (on every occasion, in every season) **in the Spirit,** with all [manner of] prayer and entreaty... (Ephesians 6:18 *AMPC*). Praying in the Spirit is drinking of the Spirit! According to these scripture passages, what happens to you when you pray in the language of the Spirit?

    *   1 Corinthians 14:2,4,14,15

    *   Romans 8:26,27

    *   Jude 1:20

PRACTICAL APPLICATION

But be ye doers of the word, and not hearers only,
deceiving your own selves.
— James 1:22

1. Do you know someone who has been under the influence of excessive alcohol? How would you describe their behavior? How were their actions different from when they were sober?

2. God's instruction through Paul — to not be drunk with wine — doesn't just apply to alcohol consumption. It involves anything of this world that would try to take God's rightful place of priority in your life. Take a moment to pray, *"Lord, is there anything of this world that I have a tendency to be 'drunk' with that is negatively impacting my thinking and behavior? If so, what is it?*

3. Did God show you something detrimental that you're drinking of excessively? Take a moment to *repent* and ask for His forgiveness. Then ask Him to give you the power and desire to be filled with His Spirit. What adjustments can you make in your daily routine to make time to drink in more of the Holy Spirit?

4. Have you become like an old wineskin — dry, hardened, and inflexible? God can make you new again if you are willing to submit to His dealings. Take time now to pray as David did:

   "Purge me with hyssop, and I shall be clean: wash me, and I shall be whiter than snow.... Create in me a clean heart, O God; and renew a right spirit within me. Cast me not away from thy presence; and take not thy Holy Spirit from me. Restore unto me the joy of thy salvation; and uphold me with thy free spirit" **(Psalm 51:7,10-12).**

TOPIC

15 Symbols of the Holy Spirit

SCRIPTURES

1. **2 Corinthians 1:21** — Now he which stablisheth us with you in Christ, and hath anointed us, is God.

2. **Psalm 133:1-3** — Behold, how good and how pleasant it is for brethren to dwell together in unity! It is like the precious ointment upon the head, that ran down upon the beard, even Aaron's beard: that went down to the skirts of his garments; as the dew of Hermon, and as the dew that descended upon the mountains of Zion: for there the Lord commanded the blessing, even life for evermore.

3. **Joel 2:23** — Be glad then, ye children of Zion, and rejoice in the Lord your God: for he hath given you the former rain moderately, and he will cause to come down for you the rain, the former rain, and the latter rain in the first month.

4. **Joel 2:28-29** — And it shall come to pass afterward, that I will pour out my Spirit upon all flesh; and your sons and your daughters shall prophesy, your old men shall dream dreams, your young men shall see visions: and also upon the servants and upon the handmaids in those days will I pour out my Spirit.

5. **John 7:37,38** — In the last day, that great day of the feast, Jesus stood and cried, saying, If any man thirst, let him come unto me, and drink. He that believeth on me, as the scripture hath said, out of his belly shall flow rivers of living water.

6. **Isaiah 44:3 (*NIV*)** — For I will pour water upon the thirsty land, and streams on the dry ground; I will pour out my Spirit on your offspring, and my blessing on your descendants.

7. **1 Corinthians 12:13** — For by one Spirit are we all baptized into one body, whether we be Jews or Gentiles, whether we be bond or free; and have been all made to drink into one Spirit.

8. **Matthew 3:11** — I indeed baptize you with water unto repentance: but he that cometh after me is mightier than I, whose shoes

I am not worthy to bear: he shall baptize you with the Holy Ghost, and with fire.

9. **Matthew 3:16** — And Jesus, when he was baptized, went up straightway out of the water: and, lo, the heavens were opened unto him, and he saw the Spirit of God descending like a dove, and lighting upon him.

10. **Luke 24:49** — And, behold, I send the promise of my Father upon you: but tarry ye in the city of Jerusalem, until ye be endued with power from on high.

11. **Acts 2:2** — And suddenly there came a sound from heaven as of a rushing mighty wind, and it filled all the house where they were sitting.

12. **Acts 2:38** — Then Peter said unto them, Repent, and be baptized every one of you in the name of Jesus Christ for the remission of sins, and ye shall receive the gift of the Holy Ghost.

13. **Ephesians 1:13,14** — In whom ye also trusted, after that ye heard the word of truth, the gospel of your salvation: in whom also after that ye believed, ye were sealed with that holy Spirit of promise, which is the earnest of our inheritance until the redemption of the purchased possession, unto the praise of his glory.

14. **1 Peter 4:14** — If ye be reproached for the name of Christ, happy are ye; for the spirit of glory and of God resteth upon you: on their part he is evil spoken of, but on your part he is glorified.

15. **2 Corinthians 4:6** — For God, who commanded the light to shine out of darkness, hath shined in our hearts, to give the light of the knowledge of the glory of God in the face of Jesus Christ.

16. **Ephesians 5:18** — And be not drunk with wine, wherein is excess; but be filled with the Spirit.

GREEK WORDS

There are no Greek words for this lesson.

SYNOPSIS

Without question, the Holy Spirit is amazing! He is the third person of the trinity, who is fully God and lives inside of us as believers. He loves you intensely and longs to be welcome in every aspect of your life. In the previous nine lessons, we have seen that throughout the Old and New Testament, there are numerous symbols or metaphors that are used to describe how the Spirit works in our lives. The more you come to know and understand these symbols, the richer and more meaningful your life will be.

The emphasis of this lesson:

In this lesson, we will quickly review the 15 symbols of the Holy Spirit we have examined in this series. These include the Holy Spirit's manifestation as oil, dew, rain, a river, water, fire, a dove, clothing, wind, a gift, a seal, an earnest, glory, light, and wine.

1. OIL

The first symbol we saw of the Holy Spirit in both the Old and the New Testament is anointing *oil*. It appears more than 200 times and is the most widely used metaphor of the Holy Spirit in the Bible. The word "anointed" is from the Greek word *chrió*, which means *to anoint with oil*. The word *chrió* is a form of the Greek word for *the human hand* — the word *cheira*. Hence, the word "anointing" pictures God putting His hands on us and massaging the oil of the Holy Spirit deeply into our lives.

This truth is illustrated in Second Corinthians 1:21, where the apostle Paul writes, "Now he which stablisheth us with you in Christ, and hath anointed us, is God." This verse tells us that the moment we get saved, God lays His hands on our life and places the Holy Spirit into us, and we are anointed with oil of the Spirit. From that point on, He is with us to the end of our life.

2. DEW

The second symbol of the Holy Spirit we examined is *dew*, and this is clearly seen in Psalm 133:1-3, which says: "Behold, how good and how pleasant it is for brethren to dwell together in unity! It is like the precious ointment upon the head, that ran down upon the beard, even Aaron's beard: that went down to the skirts of his garments; as the *dew* of Hermon, and as the *dew* that descended upon the mountains of Zion: for there the Lord commanded the blessing, even life for evermore."

The word "dew" in this passage is talking about *the anointing of the Holy Spirit*. It is saying that the Holy Spirit functions like "dew." Just as there is always moisture in the air, the Holy Spirit is always with us. Although we may not see or sense His presence, He is present in our churches, our homes, and our lives. And just as the invisible moisture in the air suddenly becomes visible on everything when the atmospheric conditions are right, the Holy Spirit suddenly begins to manifest and touch everyone present when God's people come together in unity. Hence, *unity* in the Church is like the dew point. When God's people are unified, the corporate anointing is released touching everyone assembled.

3. RAIN

Rain is the third symbol of the Holy Spirit we looked at, and it is described in Joel 2:23, which says, "Be glad then, ye children of Zion, and rejoice in the Lord your God: for he hath given you the former rain moderately, and he will cause to come down for you the rain, the former rain, and the latter rain in the first month."

In Israel, the *early rain* was the first rain, and it usually occurred in October and November. It softened and prepared the soil, making possible the germination of the seed that had been planted. The *latter rain* was equally important. It usually came between March and April, and it was essential for bringing crops to full maturity so they could be harvested.

Symbolically, the outpouring of the Holy Spirit on the Day of Pentecost was the *early rain*, which is prophesied in Joel 2:28 and 29. God was preparing the soil of the souls of men to receive the preaching of the Gospel. A greater outpouring, or *latter rain*, has already begun, and will continue to increase as we draw closer and closer to the rapture of the Church.

4. A RIVER

The fourth symbol of the Holy Spirit was made known to us by Jesus Himself. The Bible says, "In the last day, that great day of the feast, Jesus stood and cried, saying, If any man thirst, let him come unto me, and drink. He that believeth on me, as the scripture hath said, out of his belly shall flow rivers of living water" (John 7:37,38).

The word "flow" in verse 38 is the Greek word *rheo*, and it pictures *a mighty rushing stream that is so full it overflows its banks*. Jesus said the Holy Spirit is a stream overflowing with "living water," which is a translation of the Greek words *hudatos zontos*, and it describes *water that is living; water filled with vibrancy and life*. Here, Jesus Himself is comparing the refreshing, life-giving work of the Holy Spirit with a mighty, rushing river that is highly-oxygenated and is teeming with life.

And just as there are different types of rivers, there are also different types of moves of the Holy Spirit. Sometimes He is noisy when He moves, like a shallow river. Other times, He does a deep, quiet work and resembles a deep river. One thing is certain: the river of the Spirit will remove every resisting force it needs to in order to flood us with His divine life.

5. WATER

Water is the fifth symbol of the Holy Spirit in Scripture. In Isaiah 44:3 (*NIV*), God said, "For I will pour water upon the thirsty land, and streams on the dry ground; I will pour out my Spirit on your offspring, and my blessing on your descendants."

The apostle Paul also used the metaphor of *water* in First Corinthians 12:13 when he said, "For by one Spirit are we all baptized into one body, whether we be Jews or Gentiles, whether we be bond or free; and have been all made to *drink* into one Spirit."

Notice he said we "have been all made to drink into one Spirit." The word "drink" is the Greek word *potidzo*, which means *to drink, to consume*, or *to be irrigated*. By using this word, God is saying, "If you're thirsty or hungry for more of Me, I will pour out My Spirit on you like water. Even if your soul feels like parched ground, I will irrigate you and revive you with My Spirit, so you can once again produce fruit."

6. FIRE

The sixth symbol of the Holy Spirit we discovered is *fire*. John the Baptist talked about this aspect of the Spirit in all four gospels. For instance, in Matthew 3:11, he said, "I indeed baptize you with water unto repentance: but he that cometh after me is mightier than I, whose shoes I am not worthy to bear: he shall baptize you with the Holy Ghost, and with fire." The person that John referred to who was coming after him was Jesus. He is the One who baptizes us with the Holy Spirit and fire!

What does fire do? It illuminates the darkness, burns up rubbish, and is used to purify our environment. In the same way, when the Holy Spirit begins to work in our lives, He brings His holy *fire* to purify our hearts and minds, incinerate all the rubbish in our lives, and illuminate the darkness with truth.

Furthermore, just as fire is used to empower engines, the Holy Spirit's *fire* empowers us for God's service. In Acts 2:2, when the disciples were filled with the Holy Spirit, cloven tongues of *fire* settled on each of them.

These men who were once terrified to step outside the Upper Room were set ablaze with the spiritual *fire* of the Holy Spirit. Energized by divine fire, they began to boldly take the Gospel to the ends of the earth. We too need the *fire* of the Holy Spirit.

7. A DOVE

How else is the Holy Spirit depicted in Scripture? The Bible says that He also comes like *a dove*. We see this clearly in Matthew 3:16, which says, "And Jesus, when he was baptized, went up straightway out of the water: and, lo, the heavens were opened unto him, and he saw the Spirit of God descending like a dove, and lighting upon him."

Of course, we know the Holy Spirit is not a bird with feathers that flies around. The Scripture uses the phrase "like a dove" to describe the gentleness and tenderness of the Holy Spirit as He works in our lives. He is loving and caring in the way He speaks to us and corrects us. His methods are calm and soothing like that of a dove.

8. CLOTHING

The eighth symbol of the Holy Spirit is *clothing*, and Jesus described this manifestation to His disciples just before ascending into Heaven. In Luke 24:49, He said, "And, behold, I send the promise of my Father upon you: but tarry ye in the city of Jerusalem, until ye be endued with power from on high."

We saw that the word "endued" in this verse is the Greek word *enduo*, which means *to be clothed; to array, or to put on*. This word carries the idea of *sinking into a garment* and depicts *one who is so comfortable in his clothing, he sinks into it*.

By using this word, Jesus is saying that God's intention was never for you to have an encounter with His divine power and then lose it. On the contrary, He intended for you to settle into His power and for it to become such a regular part of your life that you are clothed in His Spirit habitually. The power of the Holy Spirit is to be every believer's new surroundings.

9. WIND

Wind is the ninth symbol of the Holy Spirit we learned about, and like fire, it, too, is clearly depicted on the Day of Pentecost when the Spirit descended on the disciples in the Upper Room. Acts 2:2 says, "And suddenly there came a sound from heaven as of a rushing mighty *wind*, and it filled all the house where they were sitting."

We saw that the word "sound" in this verse is the Greek word *echos*, which describes *the deafening roar of the sea*. If you've ever been caught in a storm, you know how loud it can be. It can be so deafening that you have to yell to the person next to you so they can hear what you're trying to say. That is the intensity of the noise being described by the Greek word *echos* — translated here as "sound."

Another important word in this verse is the word "mighty." It is the Greek word *biaias*, which describes *something violent*. The sound of the Holy Spirit's arrival thundered like the roaring of a sea. When He descended in the Upper Room on the Day of Pentecost, there was nothing quiet about it. In fact, it was quite deafening. Like a rushing mighty wind, the Spirit filled the whole house, which means no one could escape from the sound of it. Although they couldn't see the Spirit because He came like *wind*, they could hear Him and feel the effects of His presence.

The same is true for you. Although you can't see the Holy Spirit, you can feel and see the effects of His presence when He begins to move. Just as tornadic winds are so powerful they can change the earth's topography, when the Holy Spirit begins to move like *wind* in your life, in your church, or in your nation, He comes with such a powerful force He can reshape the spiritual landscape.

10. A GIFT

In Scripture, the Holy Spirit is also referred to as a *gift*. We see this clearly in Acts 2:38, which says, "Then Peter said unto them, Repent, and be baptized every one of you in the name of Jesus Christ for the remission of sins, and ye shall receive the *gift* of the Holy Ghost."

The Holy Spirit is God's *gift* to you — *a gift that is freely given and not acquired by merit or entitlement*. The question is, have you unwrapped it? If someone you know and loved gave you an extravagant gift that was exquisitely wrapped, would you just carry it around and never open it? Of course not — you would unwrap it. That's what God wants you to do with the *gift* of His Spirit. He wants you to take off all the wrappings and explore the most amazing gift you'll ever receive — the gift of His Holy Spirit.

11. A SEAL

Another powerful symbol of the Holy Spirit is that He is a *seal*. The apostle Paul described this in Ephesians 1:13, which says, "In whom ye also trusted, after that ye heard the word of truth, the gospel of your salvation: in whom also after that ye believed, ye were *sealed* with that holy Spirit of promise."

In Greek, the word "sealed" *sphragidzo*, which describes *a seal placed on a package after the product had been thoroughly examined and inspected to make sure it was fully intact and complete.* The seal was proof that the product was impeccable. It also identified who the owner of the package was and guaranteed its safe arrival at its ultimate destination. The use of this word tells us that the moment we were saved, God thoroughly inspected our hearts and found us perfect and complete in Christ. He then "sealed" us with the Holy Spirit, guaranteeing our safe entrance in Heaven.

12. AN EARNEST

The twelfth symbol of the Holy Spirit is that He is an *earnest*. Immediately after explaining that we are sealed with the Holy Spirit, the apostle Paul went on to say that the Holy Spirit is also, "…the *earnest* of our inheritance until the redemption of the purchased possession, unto the praise of his glory" (Ephesians 1:14). In Greek, the word "earnest" is the word *arrabon*, which describes *a payment given in advance to guarantee the whole amount will be paid afterward.* It denotes *earnest-money*; *an installment*; *a deposit*; or *a down-payment, which guarantees full delivery of a promise.* The fact the Holy Spirit is our "earnest" is God's promise to completely finish His work in our lives.

13. GLORY

Another amazing emblem of the Holy Spirit is that He is God's *glory.* The apostle Peter described this in his first epistle stating, "If ye be reproached for the name of Christ, happy are ye; for the spirit of *glory* and of God resteth upon you: on their part he is evil spoken of, but on your part he is glorified" (1 Peter 4:14).

We saw that the word "glory" is the Greek word *doxa*, and when it is used in the Old Testament Septuagint, it describes *the heavy weight of God's presence.* This was sometimes referred to as the Shekinah glory that could be tangibly felt, seen, and experienced. Today, when the Holy Spirit manifests as "glory," God's heavy presence fills the atmosphere and is saturated with all the treasures of His goodness. As the Spirit hovers over all who are gathered, He *discerns* every need represented, and then begins to miraculously meet those needs by distributing to each person out of His rich treasury.

14. LIGHT

The fourteenth symbol of the Holy Spirit that we examined is *light*. The Bible says, "For God, who commanded the light to shine out of darkness, hath shined in our hearts, to give the light of the knowledge of the glory of God in the face of Jesus Christ" (2 Corinthians 4:6).

The words "shine" and "shined" in this verse is the Greek word *lampo*, which means *to shine*, and it depicts *a direct beam of light*. This means, when the Holy Spirit comes and begins to "shine" His light in our lives, He focuses *a direct beam of light* on the problem that needs to be addressed.

This brings us to the word "light," which is the Greek word *photismos*. It is from where we get the word *photo*, and it describes *a light that is so intensely bright that it makes a permanent, lasting impression*. The use of this word lets us know that when the Holy Spirit shines His searchlight on our lives and on the truth of God's Word, He creates such a lasting impression that we're never the same again. Only the Holy Spirit can give us spiritual eyes to see and understand the truth and know what needs to change in our lives.

15. WINE

Last, but certainly not least, we saw that the Holy Spirit is also likened to *wine*. Writing under the inspiration of the Holy Spirit, the apostle Paul wrote, "And be not drunk with wine, wherein is excess; but be filled with the Spirit" (Ephesians 5:18). When we are filled with the Spirit, something amazing happens. Just as consuming an excessive amount of alcohol changes us, drinking of the Spirit changes us too — but in a positive way. It enlivens our faith, makes us bolder, and enables us to do and say things we couldn't normally do. Indeed, being filled with the *wine* of the Spirit has intoxicating effects that are transforming.

Friend, these are the 15 symbols of the Holy Spirit that we have explored, which appear in the Old and New Testament. As a believer, the Holy Spirit has made His permanent home inside of you, and He desires to make every expression of His character real in your life! Take time today to thank Him for His extraordinary, personal ministry to you and surrender yourself anew to His leadership in your life.

STUDY QUESTIONS

**Study to shew thyself approved unto God, a workman that needeth
not to be ashamed, rightly dividing the word of truth.**
— 2 Timothy 2:15

1. Can you think of any additional symbols of the Holy Spirit not covered in these lessons? If so, what are they? What verses of scripture do
   you know that illustrate these symbols?

2. Without question, the Holy Spirit is a priceless, indescribable gift
   we have been given! In light of this fact, what does the Bible caution
   you not to do in Ephesians 4:30; 1 Thessalonians 5:19; and Hebrews
   10:29? What specific activities do you need His strength to help you
   avoid? (Consider Ephesians 4:25-32; 1 Thessalonians 5:19,20; and
   Hebrews 10:29.)

3. Have you received the baptism in the Holy Spirit with the gift of
   speaking in tongues? If you haven't but would like to, carefully read
   Jesus' words in Luke 11:9-13. Ask Him for faith to believe in your
   heart that what you ask for is given to you the moment you ask (*see*
   James 1:6,7; Mark 11:24). Then pray and ask Jesus to baptize you in
   the Holy Spirit.

PRACTICAL APPLICATION

But be ye doers of the word, and not hearers only,
deceiving your own selves.
— James 1:22

1. Of the 15 symbols of the Holy Spirit we have explored in this series,
   which expression (or expressions) are you personally most grateful for?
   What makes this one special to you? What facet of the Holy Spirit's
   character would you like to see become more of a reality in your life?

2. In light of what you've learned in this series — along with your
   personal experiences of walking with God — how would you describe
   what you know about the Person, power, and ministry of the Holy
   Spirit?

3. We have learned some amazing things about the Holy Spirit, but just
   knowing about Him in your *head* is not the same as *knowing Him
   intimately*. Be honest: what kind of fellowship do you have with the

Holy Spirit? Is it a distant, hit-or-miss relationship? Or is it a close, ongoing connection?

4. As you complete this final lesson, take a few moments to pray this prayer:

Father, thank You for the marvelous ministry of the Holy Spirit. Thank You that when I accepted Jesus as my Savior and Lord, You laid Your hands on me and worked the anointing of the Spirit into my life. Holy Spirit, thank You for making me Your permanent home. Please remove all the hindrances that are blocking me from knowing You. Take the head knowledge You've shown me and make it a heart revelation of who You really are. I love You Lord! In Jesus' Name, Amen!

Notes

Notes

www.ingramcontent.com/pod-product-compliance
Lightning Source LLC
Chambersburg PA
CBHW060414050426
42449CB00009B/1969